Understanding Hybrid Environments in SharePoint 2019

Building and Implementing Features

Nanddeep Sadanand Nachan
Smita Sadanand Nachan

Apress®

Understanding Hybrid Environments in SharePoint 2019: Building and Implementing Features

Nanddeep Sadanand Nachan
Pune, India

Smita Sadanand Nachan
Pune, India

ISBN-13 (pbk): 978-1-4842-6049-4
https://doi.org/10.1007/978-1-4842-6050-0

ISBN-13 (electronic): 978-1-4842-6050-0

Managing Director, Apress Media LLC: Welmoed Spahr
Acquisitions Editor: Smriti Srivastava
Development Editor: Laura Berendson
Coordinating Editor: Shrikant Vishwakarma

Cover designed by eStudioCalamar

Cover image designed by Pexels

Distributed to the book trade worldwide by Springer Science+Business Media New York, 233 Spring Street, 6th Floor, New York, NY 10013. Phone 1-800-SPRINGER, fax (201) 348-4505, e-mail orders-ny@springer-sbm.com, or visit www.springeronline.com. Apress Media, LLC is a California LLC and the sole member (owner) is Springer Science + Business Media Finance Inc (SSBM Finance Inc). SSBM Finance Inc is a **Delaware** corporation.

For information on translations, please e-mail booktranslations@springernature.com; for reprint, paperback, or audio rights, please e-mail bookpermissions@springernature.com.

Apress titles may be purchased in bulk for academic, corporate, or promotional use. eBook versions and licenses are also available for most titles. For more information, reference our Print and eBook Bulk Sales web page at www.apress.com/bulk-sales.

Any source code or other supplementary material referenced by the author in this book is available to readers on GitHub via the book's product page, located at www.apress.com/978-1-4842-6049-4. For more detailed information, please visit www.apress.com/source-code.

Printed on acid-free paper

Dedicated to our parents,
Shri Sadanand Nachan and Smt Archana Nachan

— Smita Sadanand Nachan

My wife,
Mrs. Sarika Nanddeep Nachan,
and
our lovely newborn baby boy, Aditya Nanddeep Nachan

— Nanddeep Sadanand Nachan

Table of Contents

About the Authors

Nanddeep Sadanand Nachan is a Microsoft MVP (Office Apps and Services), Microsoft Certified Trainer (MCT), and technology architect with experience in Microsoft technologies, including SharePoint, MS Azure, and .NET. He has been working with SharePoint for the last 15+ years, starting with SharePoint 2007 (MOSS). He wrote the book *Mastering SharePoint Framework*. He organizes and speaks at industry seminars, conferences, and community events, including SPS, Global Microsoft 365 Developer Bootcamp, and Global Power Platform Bootcamp. He is an active contributor to Office 365 Dev Patterns and Practices on GitHub and writes articles on his blog. He is also a creative and technically sound photographer with experience in custom and specialized photography.

Smita Sadanand Nachan is a SharePoint professional with 12+ years of experience in design, implementation, configuration, and maintenance of large-scale projects. She focuses on architectural design and implementation, website design and development, and complete application development cycles, with an intense focus on SharePoint and Office 365. She is a frequent speaker at various community events, including SPS, Global Microsoft 365 Developer Bootcamp, and Global Power Platform Bootcamp. She is a travel, fashion, and food blogger.

About the Technical Reviewer

 **Vijai Anand Ramalingam** is a Microsoft MVP in Office Apps and Services, and he is an experienced Modern Workplace Architect with deep knowledge in SharePoint and Office 365. He is a blogger, author, and speaker, and he has published 1,300 blogs/articles on C# Corner. He works as a Technology Architect in Cognizant Technology Solutions, United Kingdom. Vijai has worked on Microsoft SharePoint on-premises/online, Office 365, and Azure.

Acknowledgments

If not for the initiative and zeal of my co-author, Miss Smita Nachan, this book would have not progressed beyond just an idea and a notion.

I would like to thank everyone at Apress for giving us this opportunity to publish our book.

I would like to thank my parents for their endless support and for helping us in numerous ways. I would also like to thank my loving and caring wife, Mrs. Sarika Nachan, and my dear son, Aditya, who supported and encouraged me despite all the time it took me away from them. Each of them should get equal credit for bringing this book to fruition.

I would also like to thank the technical reviewer, Mr. Vijai Anand, for his vigilant reviews, suggestions, corrections, and expert opinions.

— Nanddeep Sadanand Nachan

The making of the book was a beautiful journey that I am glad I undertook. The journey spanned a few months, but the experience will last a lifetime.

I am extremely grateful to my parents, Mrs. Archana Sadanand Nachan and Mr. Sadanand Govind Nachan, for their love, prayers, caring, and for preparing me for my future. My completion of this book could not have been accomplished without the support of my family.

Finally, I extend my acknowledgment to the Apress team, especially those who helped us in many ways in reaching the completion of this book.

— Smita Sadanand Nachan

Introduction

Many organizations are now making a move to the cloud via the Office 365 platform. However, not all on-premises workloads can be migrated to the cloud for many reasons, such as business, technology, and infrastructure constraints. The concept of "hybrid" plays an important role by bringing together the best features of both worlds. We tried to bring this perspective to our readers through this book. We want to combine business needs and technical skills to create solutions that truly impact businesses. You can be the judge of how well that vision has been reached.

The primary goal in the development of this book is to create an educative book that emphasizes the core concepts of hybrid environments in SharePoint Server 2019. This book explains SharePoint hybrid concepts easily. This book contains many examples to show the working of a particular hybrid scenario. This book will help you learn the basic and advanced concepts of SharePoint hybrid environments.

Cloud technology is ever-growing and there will be more hybrid updates and capabilities released in the future. After you finish reading this book, the insight you have regarding SharePoint hybrid will enable you to set a foundation for future updates and learnings.

Who This Book Is For

For those individuals, professionals, and organizations who have started their journey to the cloud, this book will serve as a stepping stone on your way to successful mastery of a hybrid implementation. This book will be a guide for those tasked with installing, configuring, and maintaining hybrid environments with SharePoint Server 2019 for their organization. This book assumes some working knowledge of a previous release of SharePoint Server, such as SharePoint 2013 or SharePoint 2016.

How This Book Is Organized

This book is divided into 20 chapters, and it provides a detailed description of the core concepts of hybrid SharePoint. Each chapter begins with an explanation of the appropriate foundational concepts, followed by a practical implementation to reinforce the explanation. A brief description of each chapter follows.

Chapter 1: This chapter is an overview of the hybrid concept and is the foundation for the entire book. You will explore the term "hybrid," the need for a hybrid environment, some real-world use cases of hybrid implementations, and whether it's the right choice for your organization.

Chapter 2: This chapter will walk you through setting up your SharePoint Server 2019 development environment with a single server role to enable you to follow along practically in this book.

Chapter 3: This chapter provides the fundamentals of configuring SharePoint Server 2019 using AutoSPInstaller, setting up an active directory, and adding users to the active directory. Finally, you will learn to configure SharePoint Server 2019.

Chapter 4: This chapter focuses on the new user experience in SharePoint Server 2019 and compares it with the classic and SharePoint Server 2016 experiences.

Chapter 5: This chapter highlights the features that SharePoint Server 2019 brings in and leaves behind. This will help you set the platform when you configure hybrid features.

Chapter 6: This chapter covers how to configure the SharePoint Server 2019 home page in order to access information easily. The home page sets up a consistent hybrid experience for users across SharePoint Server 2019 (on-premises) and SharePoint Online (the cloud).

Chapter 7: The hybrid experience begins in earnest with this chapter. Here, you'll learn how to configure SharePoint Server hybrid and extend the workloads to SharePoint Online.

Chapter 8: This chapter describes how to register a public domain with Office 365, instead of using the default provided domain.

Chapter 9: This chapter discusses how to configure the underlying infrastructure to create a hybrid environment with SharePoint Server 2019 and Office 365.

Chapter 10: This chapter focuses on the concept of self-service site creation and new feature offerings from SharePoint Server 2019 for the self-service site creation experience.

Chapter 11: This chapter covers the concept of hybrid self-service site creation and various options available to enable the hybrid self-service site creation experience in SharePoint Server 2019.

Chapter 12: This chapter covers how to set up a hybrid taxonomy. Also, you will configure synchronization between cloud and on-premises taxonomies.

Chapter 13: This chapter covers how to set up hybrid content types. Also, you will configure synchronization between cloud and on-premises content types.

Chapter 14: This chapter covers how to configure cloud hybrid search and search the content from on-premises on SharePoint Online.

Chapter 15: This chapter describes the significance of on-premises data gateways, when to use them, installation, and configuration.

Chapter 16: This chapter covers how to integrate Power BI reporting with SharePoint Server 2019 on-premises using a data gateway.

Chapter 17: This chapter addresses how to integrate Power Apps with SharePoint Server 2019 on-premises using a data gateway.

Chapter 18: This chapter focuses on how to integrate Power Automate with SharePoint Server 2019 on-premises using a data gateway.

Chapter 19: This chapter introduces Office Online Server for SharePoint Server 2019, which allows users to read and edit Microsoft Office documents in the browser.

Chapter 20: This chapter brings in high-level scenarios of upgrading to SharePoint Server 2019 from prior SharePoint on-premises versions.

CHAPTER 1

Hybrid Overview

Many organizations are making the move to the cloud with Microsoft Office 365. However, some are not yet ready to entirely transfer their workloads to the cloud. There may be numerous reasons behind this, including organization readiness, security, and compliance. In this chapter, you will explore the term "hybrid," the need for a hybrid environment, some real-world use cases of hybrid implementations, and ways to determine if is it the right choice for your organization. The term "hybrid" means that you will get the benefits of both environments (on-premises and cloud).

Note Hybrid is not a "must" implementation. It will enable you to extend your on-premises workloads to the cloud.

The Term Hybrid

The term "hybrid" will be used throughout our discussion during this book, so let's start by discussing the term itself. In a nutshell, a hybrid is something made by combining two different elements. Let's extend this definition to the SharePoint world with these two different elements being SharePoint Server on-premises and Office 365 (Figure 1-1).

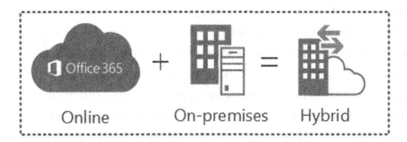

Figure 1-1. A hybrid environment Image source: docs.microsoft.com

© Nanddeep Sadanand Nachan and Smita Sadanand Nachan 2020
N. S. Nachan and S. S. Nachan, *Understanding Hybrid Environments in SharePoint 2019*,
https://doi.org/10.1007/978-1-4842-6050-0_1

Hybrids offer the best of both worlds. A SharePoint hybrid deployment is a connection between the SharePoint farm (on-premises) and Office 365 (cloud). The SharePoint farm can be hosted in your own data center, private cloud, or public cloud (MS Azure or AWS). A hybrid environment enables business users to have the greater control they need on-premises and to use the latest and greatest features in the cloud.

Need for Hybrid Environment

You might not need a hybrid environment as a common scenario. However, the following are scenarios for a hybrid environment.

Scenario 1: A phased migration approach

For any organization starting their journey to the cloud, it may not be just a lift-and-shift operation. The journey to the cloud requires a phased approach to decide the migration artifacts and carry out the actual migration. Because of several factors, including the amount of data to migrate to the cloud, complexities of the solution, and business decisions, it isn't feasible to perform the migration at one go.

In a situation like this, a hybrid environment helps to design a phased migration approach by moving the content to the cloud at your own pace and, at the same time, providing users the benefits of both environments.

Scenario 2: Leveraging existing on-premises investments

For organizations that already have huge investments in on-premises infrastructure but want to take advantage of the latest and greatest features of the cloud, a hybrid approach is a good choice.

Scenario 3: Customizations that cannot be completed in the cloud

Although the cloud provides the latest and greatest features, it offers less control than being on-premises. Due to this, some customizations cannot be completed in the cloud. Hybrid overcomes this limitation by allowing you to keep your workloads on-premises and extend other workloads to the cloud.

Scenario 4: You do not want to put some data in the cloud

Organizations care about their data. Although the cloud (or, in general, Office 365) offers all regulatory compliance solutions by implementing GDPR, multi-geo tenancy, and so on, organizations may be hesitant to move confidential data to the cloud. A hybrid approach allows that data to stay on-premises and still get the benefits of the cloud.

Benefits of Hybrid Deployments

Hybrid deployments integrate functionality and access between multiple features and services of both environments so that you can get the best of both worlds.

Here are some benefits of a hybrid deployment:

- **Control**: The key benefit of a hybrid deployment is the degree of control offered. Organizations can customize the private end of the hybrid cloud to their business needs.

- **Security**: With a hybrid environment, organizations can take advantage of the security of on-premises along with the services of the cloud.

- **Scalability**: With a hybrid deployment model, business-critical data can continue to reside on-premises but can leverage the extensive power of the cloud to effectively increase the operational capacity.

- **Integrated platforms for workloads**: The integrated platforms help things get done faster. You can add features to on-premises content with better control and also benefit from cloud offerings.

Hybrid Architecture

Here are the prerequisites for setting up a hybrid environment (also shown in Figure 1-2):

- SharePoint on-premises farm

- Office 365 license

- MS Azure subscription

- Directory federation via ADFS and Azure AD sync

- Secured communication channels

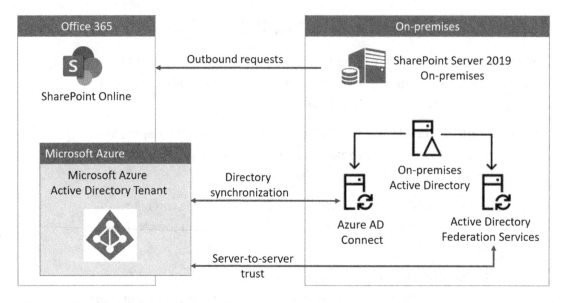

Figure 1-2. *Hybrid architecture Image source: docs.microsoft.com*

The important thing is to set up Active Directory Federation Services (AD FS) to securely share information. The single sign-on (SSO) is also handled through this.

Azure Active Directory (AAD) handles the authentication to Office 365, which also offers multi-factor authentication (MFA) and identity management. Since authentication happens via Azure AD, you must copy all of the organization's user accounts to it.

Azure Access control services handle user authentication and authorization to the web application and services.

Moving to a Hybrid Environment with SharePoint Server 2019

Microsoft has framed SharePoint Server 2019 as a "whole new generation of SharePoint." For many organizations, complex regulatory and compliance requirements make it very difficult to move their workloads to the cloud. At the same time, heavy on-premises customizations and limitations of moving the code solutions to the cloud make organizations deploy hybrid environments.

SharePoint Server 2019 offers an easy steppingstone for SharePoint-based organizations to move their workloads to the cloud. SharePoint Server 2019 eases this pain by acting as a middle ground for on-premises solutions because it offers many benefits of the cloud (SharePoint Online) as well as more control and compliance by staying on-premises.

SharePoint Server 2019 Hybrid Features

SharePoint Server 2019 offers several important features in a hybrid deployment:

- **Hybrid app launcher:** The hybrid app launcher modifies the SharePoint Server 2019 on-premises app launcher to be in synchronization with the app launcher in Office 365.

- **Hybrid sites:** The hybrid sites allow users' followed sites in both SharePoint Server 2019 on-premises and SharePoint Online to be displayed in a consolidated location, such as SharePoint home in Office 365.

- **Hybrid OneDrive for Business:** The hybrid OneDrive for Business, once enabled, allows you to create a user's OneDrive for Business in Office 365 instead of SharePoint Server 2019 on-premises.

- **Hybrid self-service site creation:** The hybrid self-service site creation allows redirection of the default self-service site creation page in SharePoint Server 2019 on-premises to SharePoint Online.

- **Hybrid auditing:** Hybrid auditing allows SharePoint administrators to push SharePoint Server 2019 on-premises audit logs to Office 365 unified audit logs.

- **Hybrid taxonomy and content types:** This feature allows for shared taxonomy and content types across SharePoint Server 2019 on-premises and SharePoint Online.

- **Hybrid business connectivity services:** This feature allows you to securely display data from an external system (e.g. SQL Server DB) without the need to connect to an on-premises environment.

- **Hybrid search:** This feature allows you to display search results from both on-premises and cloud environments in a single, consolidated place.

- **Power Platform support:** Using the on-premises data gateway, you can create Power Apps, Power Automate, and Power BI applications that can connect to on-premises content.

Conclusion

A SharePoint hybrid deployment is a connection between the SharePoint farm (on-premises) and Office 365 (in the cloud). A hybrid deployment integrates functionality and access between multiple features and services of both environments so that you can get the best of both worlds.

In the next chapter, we will cover how to set up a SharePoint Server 2019 developer VM in MS Azure.

CHAPTER 2

Setting Up SharePoint Server 2019 Developer VM in MS Azure

SharePoint Server 2019 is generally available, and it is the latest on-premises version of SharePoint. SharePoint Server 2019 is more focused on team collaboration, consistent user experience across various devices, and bringing in cloud features to the on-premises scenario. SharePoint Server 2019 is built on the same core platform as SharePoint Server 2016; however, it offers a new, modern experience to users. It also unlocks access to some features previously available only for cloud customers. This blurs the line between on-premises and cloud experiences, which facilitate a smoother transition to the cloud. SharePoint Server 2019 is a middle ground for customers looking for an on-premises solution that captures many of the benefits of SharePoint Online while giving customers the control and compliance of staying on-premises.

In this chapter, you will explore how to set up the SharePoint Server 2019 developer VM in MS Azure.

Note This chapter will walk you through setting up your SharePoint Server 2019 development environment with a single server role to enable you to follow along in this book along practically. Setting up the production environment for SharePoint Server 2019 involves planning for topology and infrastructure considerations.

© Nanddeep Sadanand Nachan and Smita Sadanand Nachan 2020
N. S. Nachan and S. S. Nachan, *Understanding Hybrid Environments in SharePoint 2019*,
https://doi.org/10.1007/978-1-4842-6050-0_2

Hardware and Software Requirements

Performing the move to SharePoint Server 2019 from previous versions of SharePoint may require several important upgrades of your hardware, operating systems, and databases, in addition to the actual software upgrade of SharePoint.

In order to set up a developer environment (single server role), here are hardware and software requirements.

Hardware Requirements

- RAM: 16GB

- Processor: 64-bit, 4 cores (for larger environments, it's best to increase CPU cores up to 8)

- Hard disk space: 80GB (system drive), 100GB (second drive)

Software Requirements

Operating system:

- Windows Server 2016/2019 Standard or Datacenter

Database:

- Microsoft SQL Server 2016/2017 RTM Standard or Enterprise Edition (64-bit version)

Prerequisites:

- Web Server (IIS) Role

- Microsoft SQL Server 2012 SP4 Native Client

- Microsoft Sync Framework Runtime v1.0 SP1 (x64)

- Windows Server AppFabric 1.1

- Microsoft Identity Extensions

- Microsoft Information Protection and Control Client 2.1

- Microsoft WCF Data Services 5.6

- Microsoft .NET Framework 4.7.2

- Cumulative Update Package 7 for Microsoft AppFabric 1.1 for
  Windows Server (KB 3092423)+

- Visual C++ Redistributable Package for Visual Studio 2012

- Visual C++ Redistributable Package for Visual Studio 2017

Microsoft Azure VM Setup Options

There are multiple options available to set up SharePoint 2019 developer VM in MS
Azure.

Note   If you do not have a MS Azure account, create your free Azure account for
12 months with a $200 credit from `https://azure.microsoft.com/free/`.

Option 1: Plain Vanilla Installation

Follow these steps to perform a plain vanilla installation:

1. Create the VM with an image of Windows Server 2016/2019
   Standard or Datacenter.

2. Install Microsoft SQL Server 2016/2017 RTM Standard or
   Enterprise Edition database.

3. Install and configure SharePoint Server 2019.

Option 2: Extend the Database Server VM

Follow these steps to perform an installation by extending the database server VM:

1. Create the VM with an image of Microsoft SQL Server 2016/2017
   RTM Standard or Enterprise Edition database.

2. Install and configure SharePoint Server 2019.

Option 3: SharePoint Server 2019 Trial VM

Follow these steps to perform an installation with SharePoint Server 2019 Trial VM:

1. Create a VM with an image of the SharePoint Server 2019 Trial.

2. Set up SQL Server 2016/2017 in the above created VM or connect to an already existing SQL server.

3. Convert the trial to a licensed version (if you have the license key).

You may choose any of the above options based on your choice of customizations, control, and time to set up the environment. However, to set up a developer environment, option 2 or 3 might be a better option.

In this chapter, you will explore option 3 by setting up a SharePoint Server 2019 trial VM.

Setting Up a SharePoint Server 2019 Trial VM in MS Azure

Follow these steps to set up a SharePoint Server 2019 Trial VM in MS Azure:

1. Open the Azure Portal (`https://portal.azure.com`)

2. From the left menu, click **Create a resource**.

3. Type in and search for **SharePoint Server Trial** in the **Search the Marketplace** search box.

4. Select **SharePoint Server Trial** as the software plan (Figure 2-1).

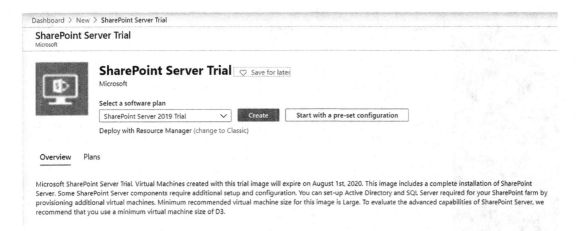

Figure 2-1. *Locating the SharePoint Server Trial VM*

5. Click the **Create** button.

6. Select a subscription. Specify resource group, virtual machine name, region, size, and other information in the wizard (Figure 2-2).

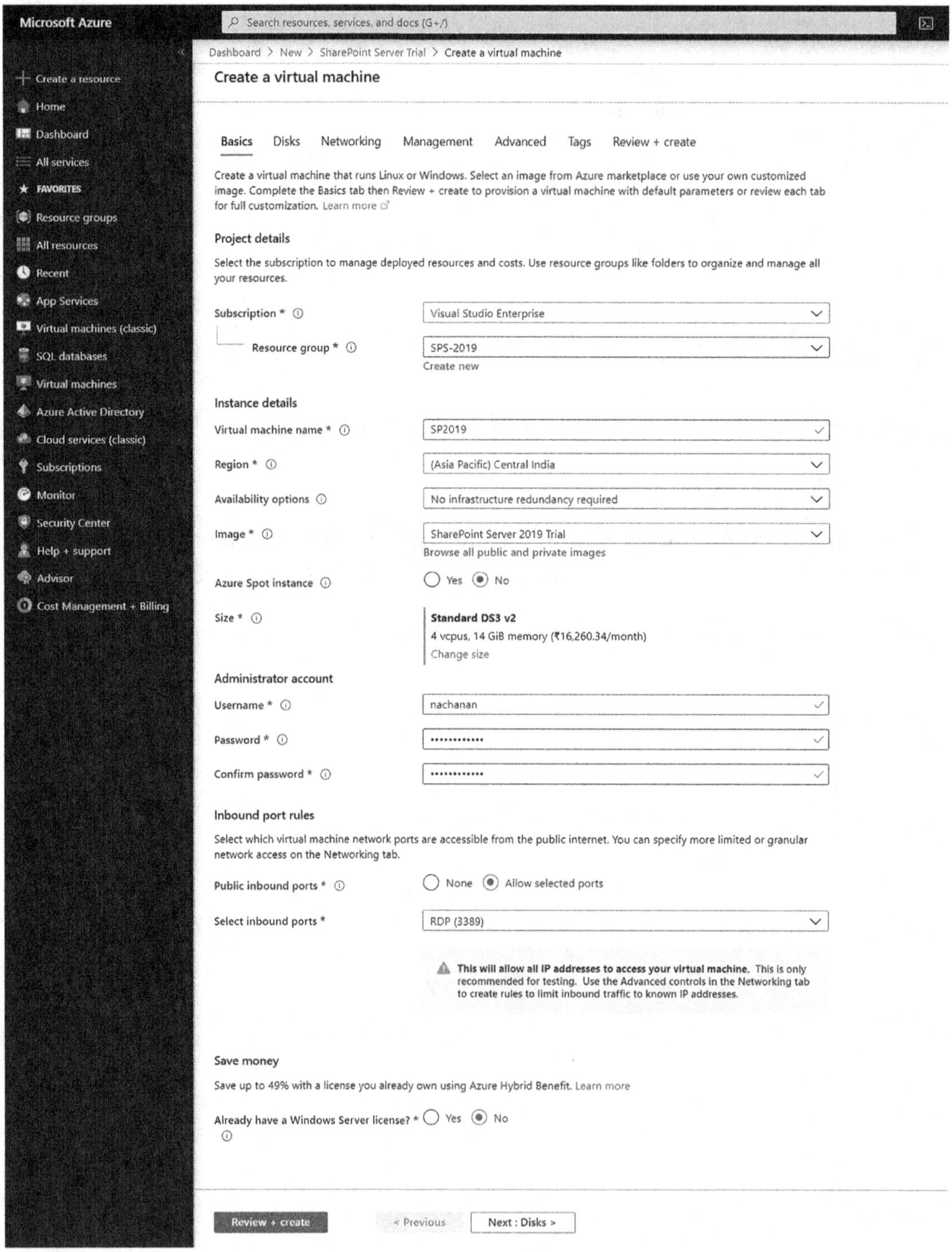

Figure 2-2. *Specifying the VM creation information*

7. Click the **Next: Disks ➤** button.

8. Select the OS disk type (Figure 2-3).

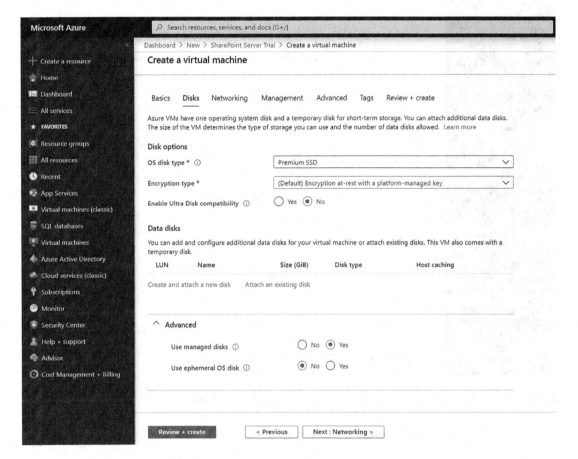

Figure 2-3. *Selecting the VM disk option*

9. Click the **Next: Networking ➤** button.

10. Specify the networking configurations (Figure 2-4).

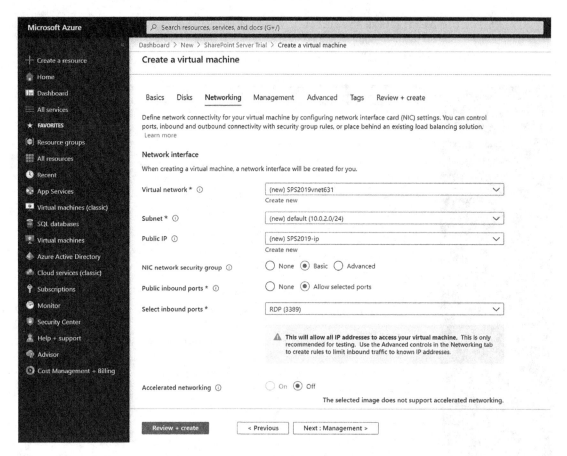

Figure 2-4. *Specifying the VM networking configurations*

11. Click the **Next: Management ➤** button.

12. Specify the monitoring options (Figure 2-5).

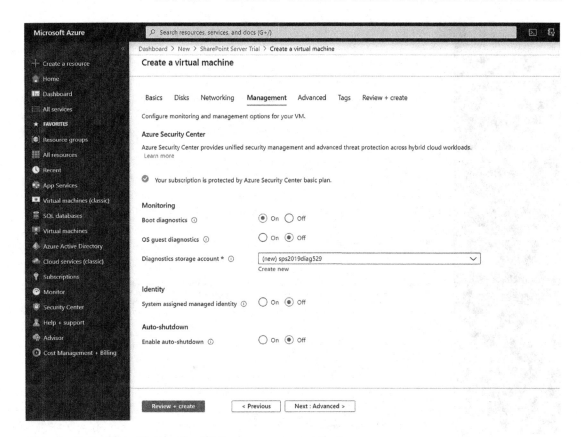

Figure 2-5. *Specifying the VM management options*

13.   Click the **Next: Advanced** ➤ button.

14.   Optionally, select any extensions to install (Figure 2-6).

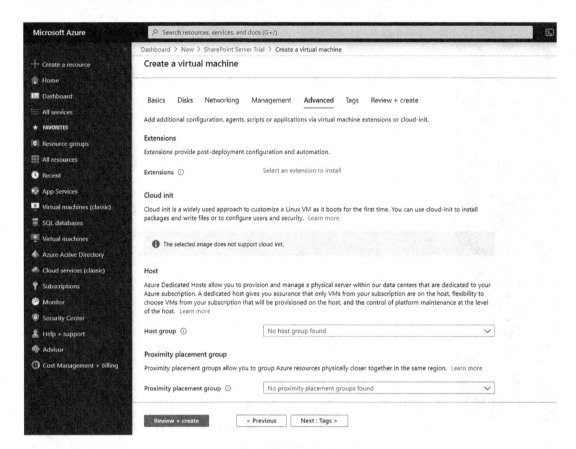

Figure 2-6. *Specifying the additional VM configurations*

15. Click the **Next: Tags ➤** button.

16. Specify any tags to categorize your resources (Figure 2-7).

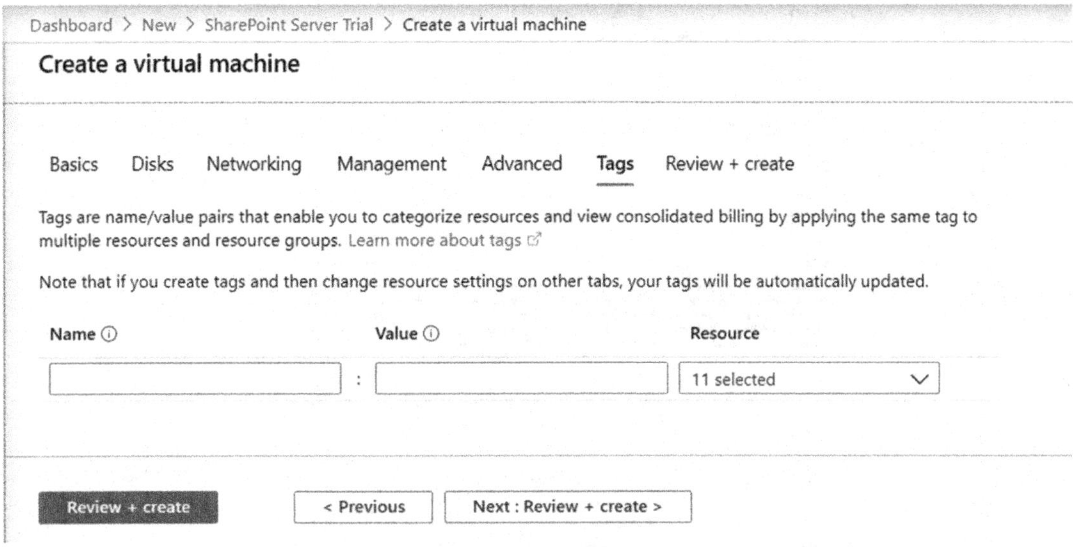

Dashboard > New > SharePoint Server Trial > Create a virtual machine

Create a virtual machine

Basics   Disks   Networking   Management   Advanced   **Tags**   Review + create

Tags are name/value pairs that enable you to categorize resources and view consolidated billing by applying the same tag to multiple resources and resource groups. Learn more about tags ⬀

Note that if you create tags and then change resource settings on other tabs, your tags will be automatically updated.

Name ⓘ		Value ⓘ	Resource
	:		11 selected ⌄

Review + create   < Previous   Next : Review + create >

Figure 2-7. Specifying tags to categorize the resources

17.   Click the **Next: Review + create ➤** button.

18.   Review the VM creation information. For any corrections, click the corresponding tab on the top to make the corrections (Figure 2-8).

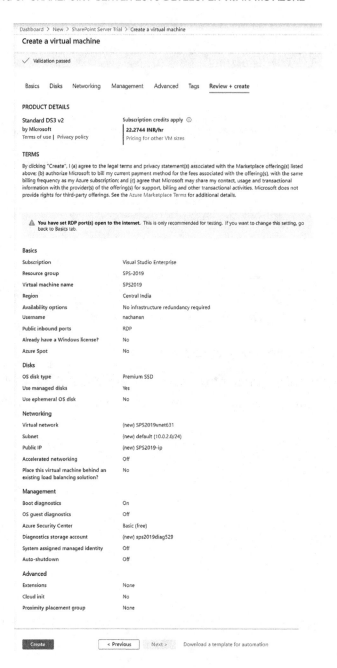

Figure 2-8. *Reviewing the VM creation information*

19.   Click the **Create** button.

20.   Once complete, the VM is ready to connect (Figure 2-9).

CreateVm-MicrosoftSharepoint.MicrosoftSharePointS-20190115012726 - Overview
Deployment

🗑 Delete   ⊘ Cancel   ⬆ Redeploy   ↻ Refresh

⊘ **Your deployment is complete**

[Go to resource]

Deployment name: CreateVm-MicrosoftSharepoint.MicrosoftSharePointS-20190115012726
Subscription: Visual Studio Enterprise
Resource group: SP2019

DEPLOYMENT DETAILS (Download)

Start time: 1/15/2019, 1:42:22 AM
Duration: 3 minutes 37 seconds
Correlation ID: af181682-7583-4428-b97b-16ba65a48e3f

RESOURCE	TYPE	STATUS	OPERATION DETAILS
⊘ SP2019	Microsoft.Compute/virtualMachines	OK	Operation details
⊘ sp2019918	Microsoft.Network/networkInterfaces	Created	Operation details
⊘ SP2019-ip	Microsoft.Network/publicIpAddresses	OK	Operation details
⊘ SP2019-nsg	Microsoft.Network/networkSecurityGroups	OK	Operation details
⊘ SP2019-vnet	Microsoft.Network/virtualNetworks	OK	Operation details

Figure 2-9. *VM deployment completion*

21. Click the **Go to resource** button.

22. Click the **Connect** button. (Figure 2-10).

Figure 2-10. *Connecting to the VM*

23. Click the **Download RDP File** button.

24. Double-click the downloaded RDP file and log in using the username and password provided during the VM creation by the wizard.

Conclusion

SharePoint Server 2019 is built on the same core platform as of SharePoint Server 2016, but it offers a new, modern experience to users. It also unlocks access to some features previously available only for cloud customers. There are multiple options available to set up a SharePoint Server 2019 farm in MS Azure. The SharePoint Server 2019 Trial VM might be a good option to start building your own SharePoint development VM in MS Azure.

In the next chapter, you will explore how to configure SharePoint Server 2019 using AutoSPInstaller, set up an active directory, and add users to the active directory.

CHAPTER 3

Configuring SharePoint Server 2019

SharePoint Server 2019 can be easily set up in MS Azure VM. Please follow the previous chapter to set up your own SharePoint Server 2019 environment in MS Azure. Once the SharePoint Server 2019 VM is ready, the next step is to configure it in order to follow the exercises from this book.

In this chapter, you will explore how to configure SharePoint 2019 using AutoSPInstaller, set up an active directory, and add users to the active directory.

Note AutoSPInstaller is an open-source set of PowerShell scripts that installs SharePoint Server 2019 and performs a base configuration for it. It can configure a single or multi-server SharePoint farm based on a predefined configuration XML file.

Setting Up an Active Directory

You will set up an AD and add the required users to it.

1. Log into SharePoint Server 2019 Trial image Azure VM.

2. Open **Server Manager**.

3. Click **Manage ➤ Add Roles and Features**.

4. Click **Server Roles**.

5. Select the **Active Directory Domain Services** role (Figure 3-1).

21

© Nanddeep Sadanand Nachan and Smita Sadanand Nachan 2020
N. S. Nachan and S. S. Nachan, *Understanding Hybrid Environments in SharePoint 2019*,
https://doi.org/10.1007/978-1-4842-6050-0_3

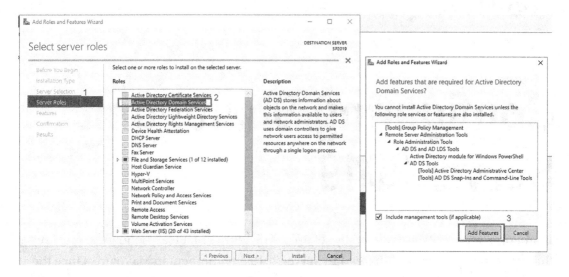

Figure 3-1. *Selecting the Active Directory Domain Services role*

6. Click **Add Features**.

7. Click **Next** until you get to the Confirmation screen (Figure 3-2).

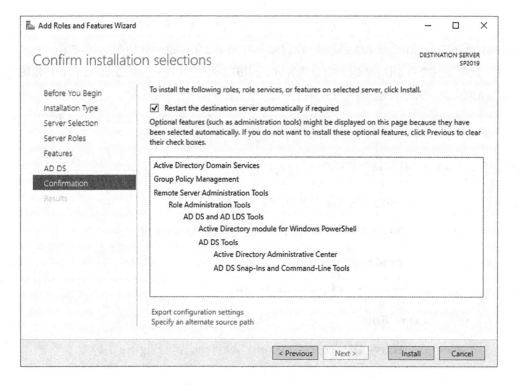

Figure 3-2. *Confirming installation selections*

8. Click **Install**.

9. Once the feature is installed, click **Close** to close the wizard.

10. Click **Promote this server to a domain controller** (Figure 3-3).

Figure 3-3. *Promoting this server to a domain controller*

11. In the deployment configuration, add a new forest (Figure 3-4).

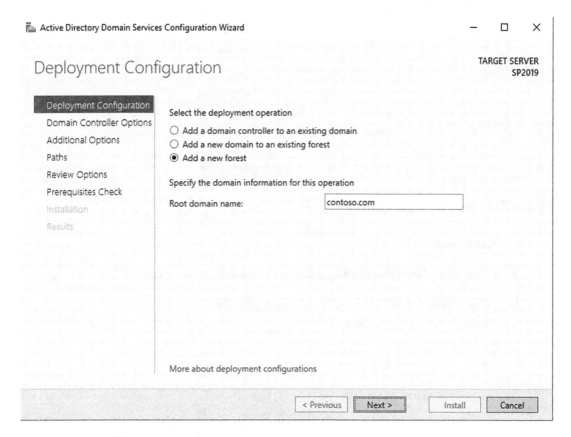

Figure 3-4. *Adding a new forest*

12.   Click **Next**.

13.   On the Domain Controller Options page, specify the DSRM
       password (Figure 3-5).

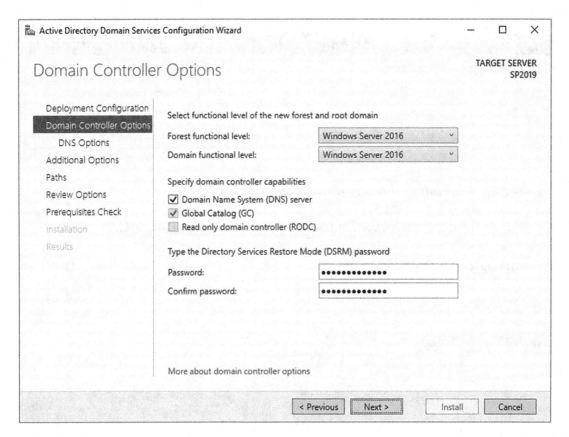

Figure 3-5. *Adding a new forest*

14.   Click **Next**.

15.   Click **Next** through the wizard to set up the active directory.

16.   Reboot the VM after it finishes installing the Active Directory
       Domain Services server role.

Setting Up AD Users

Follow these steps to set up users in an active directory:

1. Open **Server Manager**.

2. Click **Tools ➤ Active Directory Users and Computers** (Figure 3-6).

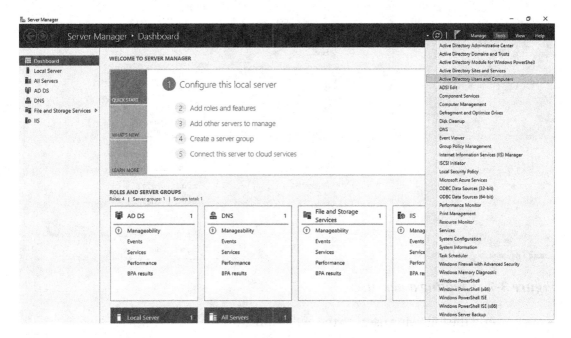

Figure 3-6. *Clicking the Active Directory Users and Computers option*

3. Create a new user (Figure 3-7).

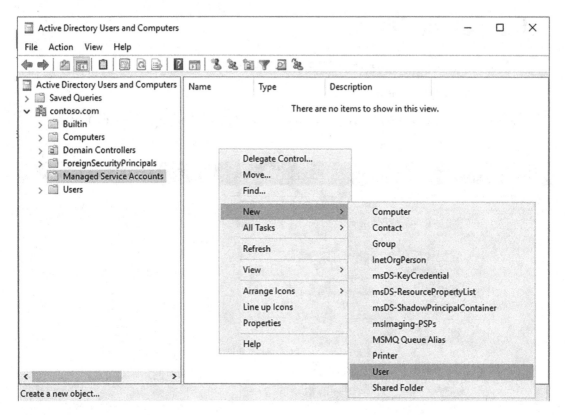

Figure 3-7. *Creating a new user*

Add the following users to the active directory:

Name	Responsibility	Local Rights	Domain Rights
sp_farm	Configure and manage the server farm. Act as the application pool identity for the SharePoint Central Administration Web site. Run the Microsoft SharePoint Foundation Workflow Timer Service.	SecurityAdmin and DB_Creator rights on the SQL Instance	Domain User

(continued)

Name	Responsibility	Local Rights	Domain Rights
sp_admin	Set up the farm via the SharePoint Products Configuration Wizard.	Local Administrator on all the SharePoint Servers. SysAdmin, SecurityAdmin, and DB_Creator rights on the SQL Instance.	Domain User
sp_PortalAppPool	The Pool account is used to run the Web Application Pools.	None	Domain User
sp_services	The Services Account is used to run the Service Application Pool.	None	Domain User
sp_crawl	The Default Content Access Account for the Search Service Application	None	Domain User
sp_SearchService	The Service Account runs the SharePoint Search "Windows Service."	Local Administrator and SysAdmin rights on the SQL instance	Domain User
sp_mysitepool	Used for the My Sites Web Application	None	Domain User
sp_ProfileSync	The User Profile Synchronization Account	None	Replicate Directory Changes permission on the domain.
wf_service	WorkFlow Manager Service Account	Local Administrator and SysAdmin rights on the SQL instance.	Domain User

(continued)

Name	Responsibility	Local Rights	Domain Rights
sp_portalsuperuser	Object Cache Service Account. The goals of the object cache are to reduce the load on the computer on which SQL Server is running and to improve request latency and throughput.	None. SharePoint: Must be an account that has full control access to the web application.	Domain User
sp_portalsuperreader	Object Cache Service Account. The goals of the object cache are to reduce the load on the computer on which SQL Server is running and to improve request latency and throughput.	None.SharePoint: Must be an account that has Full Read access to the Web application.	Domain User
sp_ExcelUser	Excel Services Application	None	Domain User
sp_VisioUser	Visio Graphics Service	None	Domain User
sp_PerfPointUser	PerformancePoint Service	None	Domain User

Configure SharePoint 2019 Using AutoSPInstaller

AutoSPInstaller is a utility for installing and configuring SharePoint. It downloads the installable binaries and prerequisites, install service packs, language packs, and cumulative/public updates.

1. Download the utility from https://autospinstaller.com/.

2. Open the **AutoSPInstallerInput.xml** file from the \AutoSPInstaller-master\SP\Automation folder.

3. Update the server and user information. Check usernames and passwords in each place they are used.

4. Once done, run **AutoSPInstallerLaunch.bat** from the \AutoSPInstaller-master\SP\Automation folder to proceed with installation and configuration (Figure 3-8).

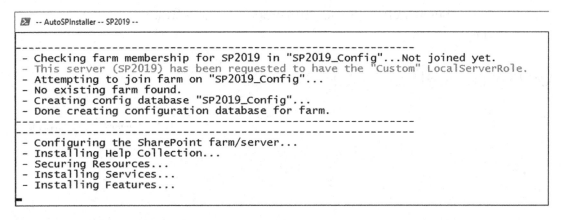

```
 -- AutoSPInstaller -- SP2019 --
----------------------------------------------------------------
 - Checking farm membership for SP2019 in "SP2019_Config"...Not joined yet.
 - This server (SP2019) has been requested to have the "Custom" LocalServerRole.
 - Attempting to join farm on "SP2019_Config"...
 - No existing farm found.
 - Creating config database "SP2019_Config"...
 - Done creating configuration database for farm.
----------------------------------------------------------------
----------------------------------------------------------------
 - Configuring the SharePoint farm/server...
 - Installing Help Collection...
 - Securing Resources...
 - Installing Services...
 - Installing Features...
```

Figure 3-8. *Configuring SharePoint 2019 using AutoSPInstaller*

Converting a SharePoint Trial to an RTM License

The SharePoint Server 2019 version installed to Azure VM is a trial version. You can convert it to RTM by following these steps:

1. Open the **SharePoint Central Administration** site.

2. Click **Convert farm license type** under **Upgrade and Migration** (Figure 3-9).

Figure 3-9. *Converting SharePoint Trial to an RTM License*

3. Enter your SharePoint Server 2019 product key to activate
    (Figure 3-10).

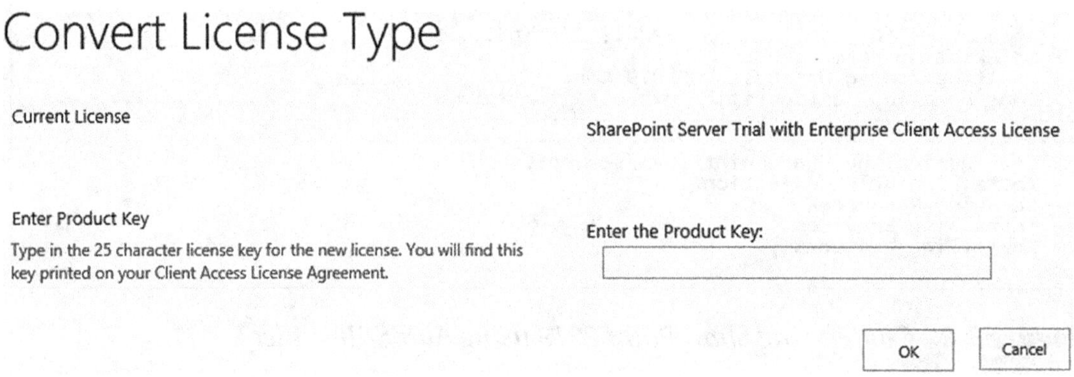

Convert License Type

Current License   SharePoint Server Trial with Enterprise Client Access License

Enter Product Key   Enter the Product Key:
Type in the 25 character license key for the new license. You will find this
key printed on your Client Access License Agreement.

[OK   ]   [Cancel   ]

Figure 3-10. Converting the license type

4. Click **OK**.

5. This will take some time. After successful validation, the license
    type is converted to RTM (standard or enterprise, based on the
    product key).

Conclusion

There are multiple options available to set up a SharePoint 2019 farm in MS Azure.
The SharePoint Server 2019 Trial VM might be a good option to start building your
own SharePoint development VM in MS Azure. The AutoSPInstaller tool downloads,
installs, and configures the SharePoint environment with granular control driven by the
AutoSPInstallerInput.xml file.

In the next chapter, you will explore the new user experience in SharePoint 2019 and
compare it with the classic and SharePoint Server 2016 experiences.

CHAPTER 4

SharePoint Server 2019 User Experience

SharePoint Server 2019 is the latest on-premises version of SharePoint as of today. It is built on the foundational release of SharePoint Server 2016. This means there are no huge architectural changes in SharePoint Server 2019 from SharePoint Server 2016. However, from the end user perspective, the experience has changed a lot. SharePoint Server 2019 has been updated to a new, modern experience. The modern experience is not new to cloud (SharePoint online) users, but it can now be experienced in SharePoint on-premises. In this chapter, you will explore the new user experience in SharePoint Server 2019 and compare it with the classic and SharePoint Server 2016 experiences.

SharePoint Server 2019 User Experience

The user experience starts right from the creation of the site, browsing the content, and managing the content.

Site Collection Creation

SharePoint Server 2019 supports the creation of both classic and modern SharePoint sites. Figure 4-1 shows the site template selection dialog of SharePoint Server 2019.

© Nanddeep Sadanand Nachan and Smita Sadanand Nachan 2020
N. S. Nachan and S. S. Nachan, *Understanding Hybrid Environments in SharePoint 2019*,
https://doi.org/10.1007/978-1-4842-6050-0_4

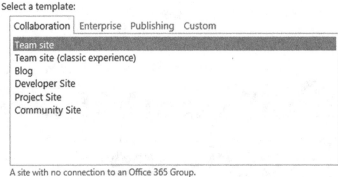

Figure 4-1. *Site collection creation*

All of the classic site templates are available along with new, modern site templates. This provision can help you quickly migrate to SharePoint Server 2019 in a classic experience and then gradually upgrade to the modern experience.

Modern User Experience

The modern user experience is responsive, fascinating, flexible, and easy to use. If you are already using the SharePoint Online version, then you will observe that several features of SharePoint Server 2019 are modern, but not all features are modern yet. Let's explore the supported modern experience in SharePoint Server 2019.

Lists and Libraries Experience

The user experience of the lists and libraries has been optimized. The ribbons have been replaced by a command bar. Figure 4-2 shows a few noticeable enhancements.

1. The command bar supports the copying and moving of files.

2. Files can be pinned at the top.

3. Filtering has a new experience.

4. A view can be changed inline without going to the list settings page explicitly. Columns can be rearranged, grouped, and filtered inline.

5. Formatting columns can be applied inline.

6. Columns can be added to the list directly.

7. You can add files as links.

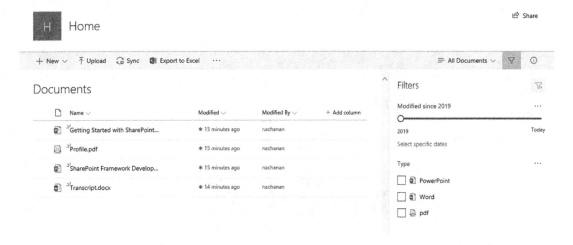

Figure 4-2. *The lists and libraries experience*

The old features (like exporting to Excel, dragging and dropping files, syncing the document library, and managing alerts) continue the same way. The lists and libraries offer a classic experience in the following scenarios:

1. The list or library settings page

2. Adding other types of columns

Team Site

Modern team sites helps to create news, show all of the news in one place, and display the site activities. Modern team sites are optimized for the mobile experience. Modern team sites support faster provisioning than classic team sites (Figure 4-3).

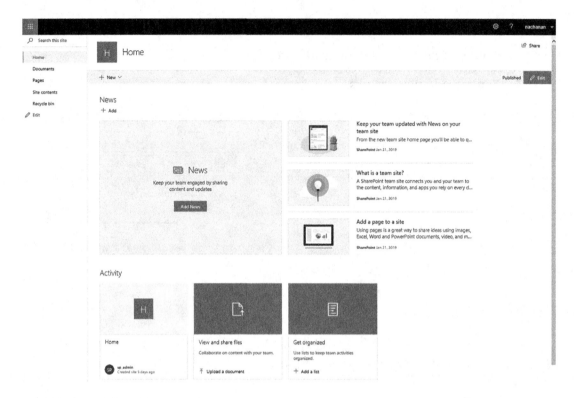

Figure 4-3. *Modern team site*

Communication Site

The modern Communication site template is available under the Publishing category (Figure 4-4).

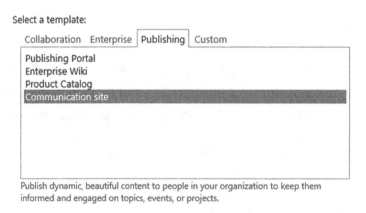

Figure 4-4. *Modern Communication site template*

A communication site shares news, events, and other information. The communication site does not rely on the publishing infrastructure (Figure 4-5).

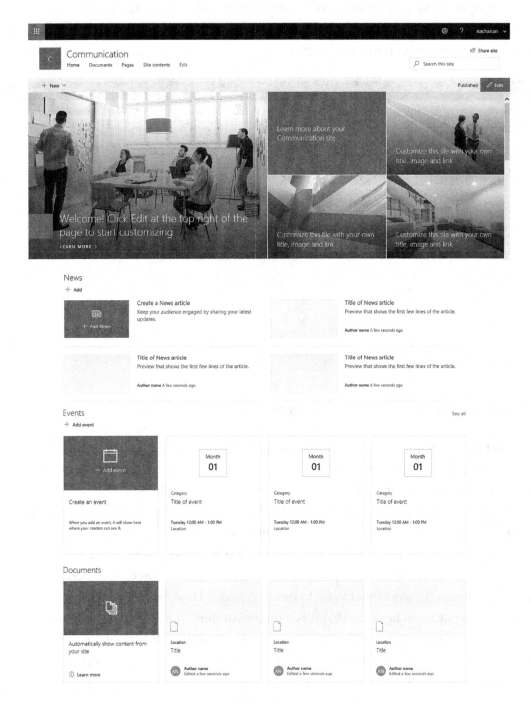

Figure 4-5. *A Modern communication site*

Pages and Web Parts

Modern pages are fast and responsive. Modern pages are less structured. The edit experience modifies the section layout, edits existing sections, and adds web parts to the page without any server postbacks (Figure 4-6).

Figure 4-6. *Modern pages and web parts*

The modern page does not have any static layout, unlike the classic page. The modern page offers a flexible layout, which can be changed at any time. Modern pages do not have any equivalent of the wiki page from classic SharePoint.

Modern pages support modern web parts (client-side web parts). For security and governance reasons, modern web parts do not allow you to add any JavaScript code to a page directly. In short, modern web parts do not include a content editor web part (CEWP) or script editor web parts. It is important to note that classic web parts are not supported or available to add to modern pages. However, the reverse is true. Modern web parts can be added to classic pages. Modern SharePoint provides a wide range of first-party web parts like Text, Quick Chart, Embed, File Viewer, Image, Spacer, Hero, News, Events, etc. The custom web parts can be created using the SharePoint Framework (SPFx).

Search Experience

SharePoint Server 2019 supports a modern search experience. The search results are shown as you type the search keyword (Figure 4-7).

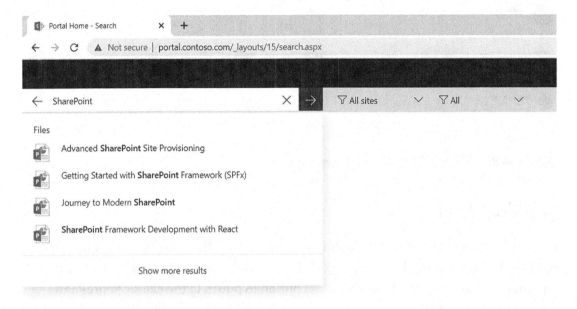

Figure 4-7. *Modern search experience*

The search results page is divided into sections named Sites, People, and Files, which display the results matching the search query. You can further apply filters from the top to narrow your search results (Figure 4-8).

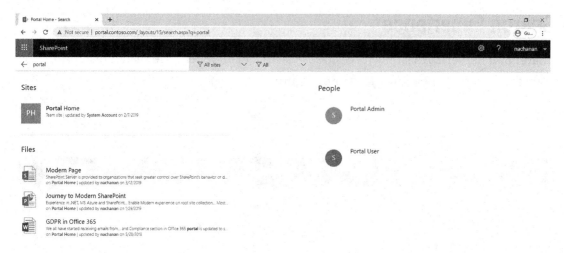

Figure 4-8. *The modern search experience*

Site Contents

The Site Contents page provides a modern experience by displaying all lists, libraries, and subsites separately. The search box at the top left corner of the page offers a search experience for site content. It also offers an option to return to the classic SharePoint experience (Figure 4-9) .

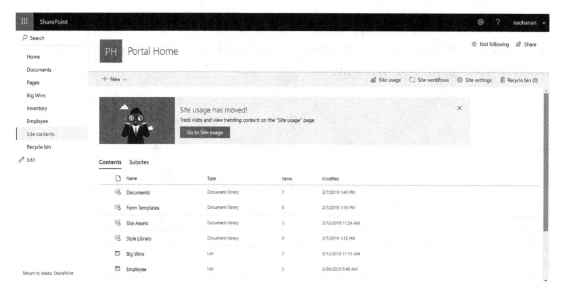

Figure 4-9. *Site contents modern experience*

Site Usage

The site usage page displays the statistics of site visits in the past seven days, new items added in the past seven days, and most viewed files during the past two weeks (Figure 4-10).

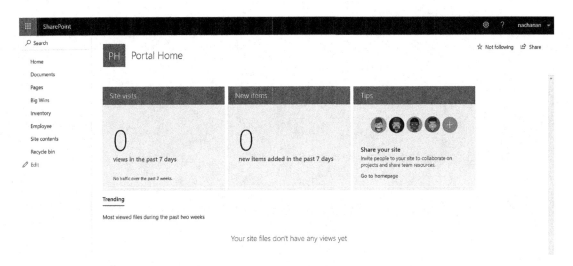

Figure 4-10. *Site usage*

Conclusion

SharePoint Server 2019 brings the modern experience to on-premises users. The SharePoint Server 2019 modern user experience is responsive, flexible, and easy to use. It supports the creation of both classic and modern SharePoint sites. SharePoint Server 2019 does not offer all of the modern experiences available in SharePoint online, however.

In the next chapter, you will explore the features that SharePoint Server 2019 brings in and leaves behind. This will help you to set the platform when you configure hybrid features.

CHAPTER 5

SharePoint Server 2019 Features Overview

Not surprisingly, SharePoint Server 2019 adds new features and leaves behind a few old features. SharePoint 2019 brings the cloud closer to the customer and the customer closer to the cloud. In other words, most of the features that were once only available within the cloud (SharePoint Online) are now available to on-premises users via SharePoint Server 2019.

In this chapter, you will explore the features that SharePoint Server 2019 adds and leaves behind. This will help you set the platform when you configure the hybrid features.

SharePoint Server 2019 Focus Areas

Microsoft says that SharePoint Server 2019 is built on the same core platform as SharePoint Online. Because of this, it brings modern experiences to the end users. SharePoint 2019 features are focused around the following areas:

- Modern experiences, as with SharePoint Online
- Responsiveness across all devices and browsers
- Enhanced hybrid scaling, security, and compliance capabilities

Improved Features

SharePoint Server 2019 supports features that users felt were lacking in SharePoint Server 2016 including the following hybrid environments:

© Nanddeep Sadanand Nachan and Smita Sadanand Nachan 2020
N. S. Nachan and S. S. Nachan, *Understanding Hybrid Environments in SharePoint 2019*,
https://doi.org/10.1007/978-1-4842-6050-0_5

- **OneDrive Sync:** SharePoint Server 2019 offers an improved OneDrive Sync app (NGSC – Next Generation Sync Client) which supports syncing files on SharePoint Server 2019 team and personal sites with your devices. It also includes push notifications. It helps to sync and share solutions like Box or Dropbox.

- **Direct links in the Central Administration site:** SharePoint Server 2019 Central Administration includes direct links to documentation, updates, etc. This will reduce searching efforts for related documentation and patching information (Figure 5-1).

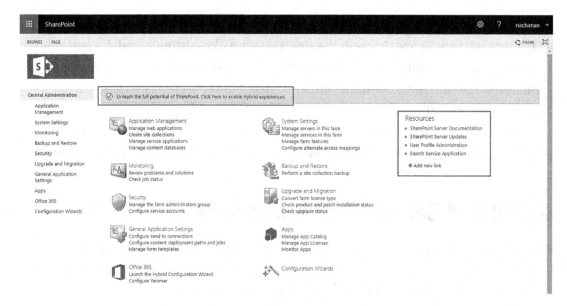

Figure 5-1. *Direct links in Central Administration*

- **Improvements in the hybrid experience:** A hybrid status bar has been added to the top area of the central administration site. If the SharePoint Server 2019 environment meets the minimum system requirements to enable a hybrid scenario, the hybrid status bar turns green and launches the SharePoint Hybrid Configuration Wizard.

- **SMTP authentication:** You can now take advantage of authenticated SMTP (including Office 365) to send emails.

- **Integration with Power Apps and Flow (Power Automate):** The cloud features of Power Apps, Power BI, and Power Automate are now available in SharePoint Server 2019. These features need to be configured via the on-premises data gateway but exist on-premises. These features help automate the business processes.

- **Communication sites:** The modern communication sites are now part of SharePoint Server 2019, which supports modern first-party web parts including the Hero web part.

- **Modern team sites:** Along with classic team sites, SharePoint Server 2019 also supports creating modern team sites, which offer a responsive user experience for better team collaboration.

- **Fast site creation:** SharePoint Server 2019 lets you create sites in a few seconds, including

  - Modern team sites

  - Communication sites

  - OneDrive personal sites

- **Increased file storage for document libraries:** SharePoint Server 2019 supports storing files up to 15GB, as compared to its predecessor, SharePoint Server 2016, which supported up to 10GB.

- **Modern list and library experience:** SharePoint Server 2019 offers a modern experience for lists and libraries similar to SharePoint Online (the cloud).

- **Modern search experience:** SharePoint Server 2019 supports a modern search experience. The search results are shown as you type the search keyword.

- **File improvements for sync:** SharePoint Server 2019 now supports # and % characters in file and folder names, thereby enabling easier sync of content from personal storage devices to the SharePoint. It also now supports an increased file path limit of 400 characters. This enables syncing of deeply nested content from personal storage devices to the SharePoint.

Depreciated and Removed Features

There are plenty of new features in SharePoint Server 2019, but it is also time to say goodbye to some old features.

Depreciated Features

The depreciated features are supported by Microsoft at the moment. However, they may be removed in future major releases. Here are a few depreciated features from SharePoint Server 2019:

- **Aggregate newsfeed:** The SharePoint newsfeed feature was helpful to start a conversation with users. The Start a conversation box to type the message will be no longer available (Figure 5-2).

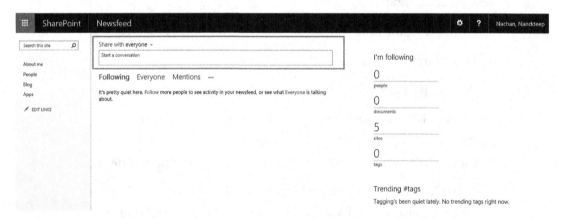

Figure 5-2. *Aggregate newsfeed*

Also, the tile in the app launcher will no longer be available (Figure 5-3).

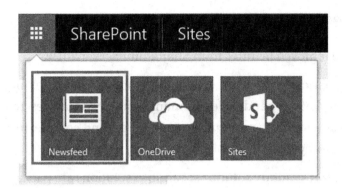

Figure 5-3. *Tile in the app launcher*

- **Hub sites:** Hub sites share things like navigation, logo, and themes across connected sites. Also, they roll up news and activities from connected sites into one place. Unfortunately, this feature did not make it into the on-premises release and is available only in SharePoint online.

- **Custom help:** The on-premises help engine synchronizes data with Office 365.

- **SharePoint Designer:** Once again there will not be a new rollout of SharePoint Designer for SharePoint Server 2019. However, Microsoft says that SharePoint Designer 2013 will work with SharePoint 2019 for the remainder of the client support lifecycle (by year 2026).

- **Visio services:** Visio services use PNG-based or Microsoft Silverlight-based rendering. Silverlight support is ending by October 2021. Because of this reason, the Silverlight-based rendering option will not be supported in SharePoint Server 2019.

- **Access Services:** Access Services 2010 and 2013 are depreciated. It is recommended to use Power Apps and Power Automate as alternatives.

- **InfoPath services:** InfoPath services are set to depreciate by 2026. There will not be a new InfoPath client. The InfoPath 2013 client will continue to work with SharePoint Server 2019 in a depreciated mode.

- **Groove sync app:** With the introduction of a new OneDrive Sync app (Next Generation Sync Client), the Groove sync app is now deprecated.

Removed Features

Here are few of the removed features from SharePoint Server 2019:

- **Multi-tenancy:** Multi-tenancy is being promoted in SharePoint Online and has dependencies on many cloud technologies, making it expensive to bring on-premises. Due to cost and complexity issues, multi-tenancy is not available in SharePoint Server 2019.

- **Code-based sandbox solutions:** Sandbox solutions are packages targeted to a specific site collection in SharePoint. They were depreciated earlier and then discarded from SharePoint Online. They have also been removed from SharePoint on-premises versions. Microsoft recommends the SharePoint add-in model or SharePoint Framework-based solutions as an alternative for custom development.

- **PDF viewer:** The built-in PDF viewer feature has been removed. Users can rely upon the native PDF rendering capabilities of modern web browsers.

- **Tags and Notes:** The Tags and Notes feature has been removed from SharePoint Server 2019. Users cannot create new tags and notes or access existing ones.

- **Visio services (Silverlight):** Visio supports rendering based on Silverlight and PNG. Since Silverlight is being depreciated by October 2021, SharePoint Server 2019 will not support Silverlight-based Visio rendering.

Conclusion

SharePoint Server 2019 does not deviate much from its predecessor, SharePoint Server 2016. However, it brings cloud features on-premises to some extent. SharePoint Server 2019 offers modern experiences, responsiveness, and enhanced hybrid, scaling, security, and compliance capabilities.

In the next chapter, you will explore how to configure the SharePoint Server 2019 home page and why it is beneficial to be able to access the information easily. The home page help is used to set up a consistent hybrid experience for users across SharePoint Server 2019 (on-premises) and SharePoint Online (the cloud).

CHAPTER 6

Configuring the Home Page in SharePoint Server 2019

SharePoint provides the flexibility to set up sites based on business scenarios and technical architecture by defining a site structure. The site structure can span from setting up web applications to creating site collections and subsites under it.

As users, we are part of multiple sites with a variety of permission sets. We contribute content to multiple sites and follow or like content from others. There are a few sites or links frequently used by us. All this information should be seen in one place for better collaboration. SharePoint Server 2019 helps collocate the information together at one place called the home page

In this chapter, you will explore how to configure the SharePoint Server 2019 home page and why it is beneficial to be able to access the information easily. The home page help can be used to set up a consistent hybrid experience for users across SharePoint Server 2019 (on-premises) and SharePoint Online (the cloud).

SharePoint Home

SharePoint home is a new feature of SharePoint Server 2019. Home is a modern page that provides a personalized experience for the users. It helps users find and access their content across multiple SharePoint sites, see activity from the sites they follow, and get news across sites.

SharePoint Server 2016 (the previous SharePoint on-premises environment) provided the Sites.aspx experience. This experience was limited to showing only sites you follow and suggested sites to follow (Figure 6-1).

© Nanddeep Sadanand Nachan and Smita Sadanand Nachan 2020
N. S. Nachan and S. S. Nachan, *Understanding Hybrid Environments in SharePoint 2019*,
https://doi.org/10.1007/978-1-4842-6050-0_6

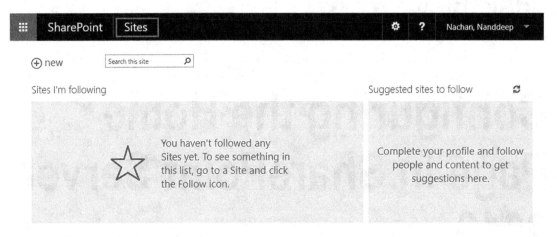

Figure 6-1. *SharePoint Server 2016 home page*

SharePoint Server 2019 replaces the Sites.aspx experience with the home page. The site tile in the app launcher is also renamed to SharePoint (Figure 6-2).

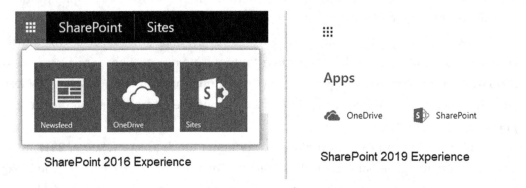

Figure 6-2. *SharePoint Server 2019 app launcher compared with SharePoint Server 2016*

To access the SharePoint Server 2019 home page,

1. Click **SharePoint** from the **App Launcher**, or

2. Click **SharePoint** from the ribbon section (Figure 6-3).

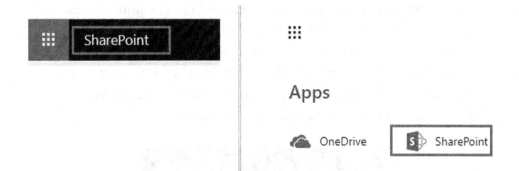

Figure 6-3. *SharePoint Server 2019 app launcher*

Features of the Home Page

Here are some of the important features of the home page:

- **Search box:** When the user clicks in the search box, a list of best-match sites and content is available immediately (Figure 6-4).

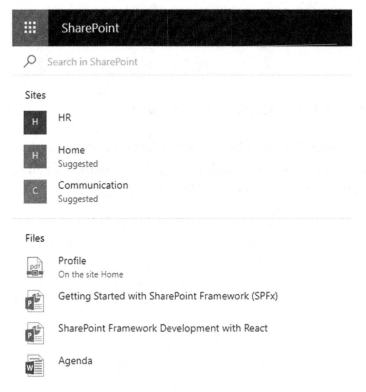

Figure 6-4. *SharePoint Server 2019 search experience*

- **Featured Links:** All important and useful links can be stored at this centralized location. Administrators of the My Site host site can set the featured links. The featured links are stored in a hidden list at /Lists/SharePointHomeOrgLinks/AllItems.aspx. Make sure that default groups are set on the My site host. If not set, then set them from /_layouts/15/permsetup.aspx (Figure 6-5).

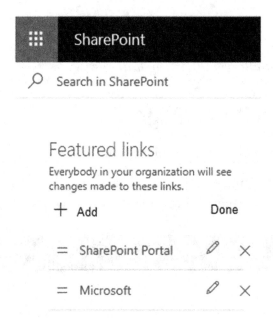

Figure 6-5. *SharePoint Server 2019 featured links*

- **Create a Site:** The SharePoint Server 2019 home page offers self-service site creation. It helps you create modern team and communication site collections (Figure 6-6).

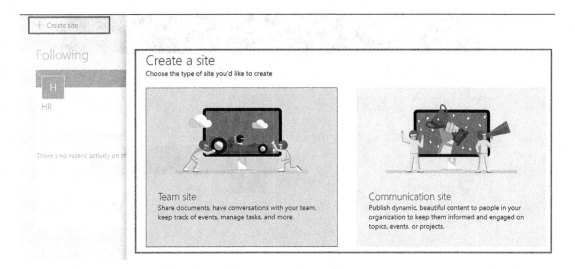

Figure 6-6. *The SharePoint Server 2019 create-a-site experience*

- **News from sites:** This section shows the latest news from followed and suggested sites (Figure 6-7).

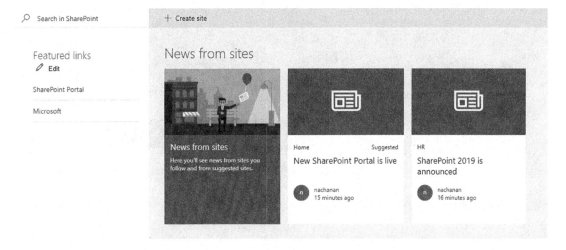

Figure 6-7. *The SharePoint Server 2019 news-from-sites experience*

- **Following Sites:** Displays the sites you follow in a tiled manner.

- **Suggested Sites:** Displays the sites you may not have seen yet, but are used by people around you (Figure 6-8).

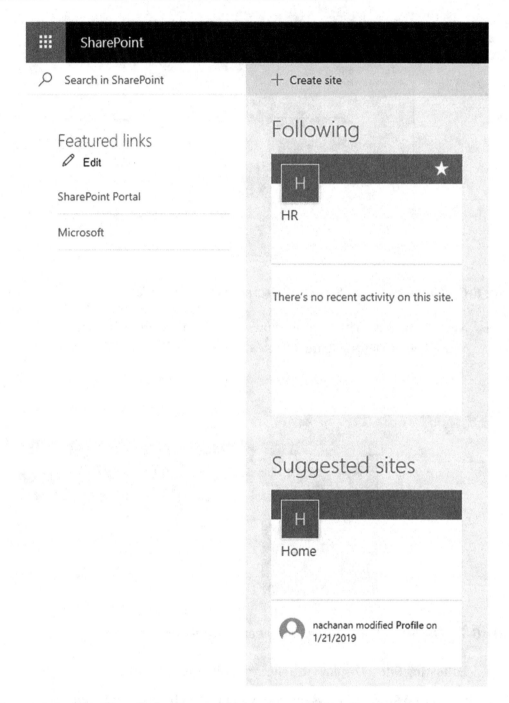

Figure 6-8. *The SharePoint Server 2019 suggested sites feature*

Supporting Services

The SharePoint Server 2019 home page is composed of various functionalities. They require certain services (service applications) in SharePoint to be created and configured:

1. Managed Metadata Service application

2. Search Service application

3. Enterprise Search Center site

4. My Site Host site

5. User Profile Service application

6. Import profiles from Active Directory, if required

7. Distributed cache (optional)

The SharePoint home page will look different to each user depending upon their activities and sites being followed. Each user should have a user profile present in the user profile service application. The search service application should be configured and set to crawl the sites.

Conclusion

The SharePoint Server 2019 home page is a new feature that displays consolidated information about the sites followed by a user, suggestions for new sites to follow, and news from all followed and suggested sites in one place. In the next chapter, you will explore how to configure a hybrid SharePoint Server scenario and extend the workloads to SharePoint Online.

CHAPTER 7

Enabling a Hybrid Experience

The SharePoint on-premises and SharePoint Online environments present advantages and features to users. The SharePoint Online environment offers services to handle business needs, and the SharePoint on-premises environment offers flexibility and more configuration options. For organizations that are gradually moving towards the cloud, a hybrid SharePoint Server setup provides a staged migration path. It helps to extend workloads to SharePoint Online.

In this chapter, you will explore how to configure a hybrid SharePoint deployment and extend workloads to SharePoint Online.

Hybrid SharePoint

A hybrid SharePoint setup brings together the best of SharePoint on-premises and SharePoint Online (the cloud) features. The hybrid environment enables trusted communication between SharePoint on-premises and SharePoint Online. It integrates functionality and access between features and services of both environments.

Enabling the Hybrid Experience in SharePoint Server 2019

Follow these steps to enable the hybrid experience:

1. Open the **SharePoint Server 2019 Central Administration** site.

2. Click the **Click here to enable Hybrid experiences** link from the green tooltip (Figure 7-1).

© Nanddeep Sadanand Nachan and Smita Sadanand Nachan 2020
N. S. Nachan and S. S. Nachan, *Understanding Hybrid Environments in SharePoint 2019*,
https://doi.org/10.1007/978-1-4842-6050-0_7

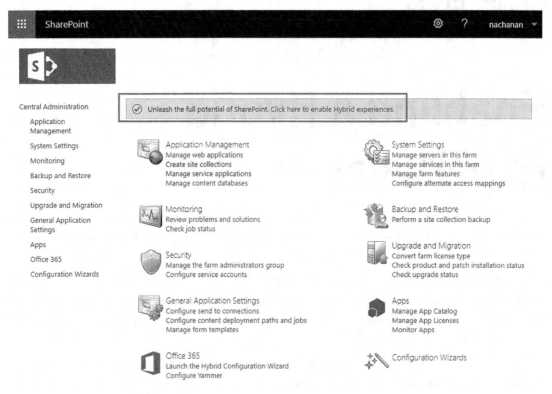

Figure 7-1. Downloading HybridSPSetup.exe

3. An executable file named HybridSPSetup.exe will be downloaded to the file system.

4. Double-click HybridSPSetup.exe to install.

5. The wizard will open to connect your on-premises SharePoint Server farm with your Office 365 tenant.

6. Click **Next** (Figure 7-2).

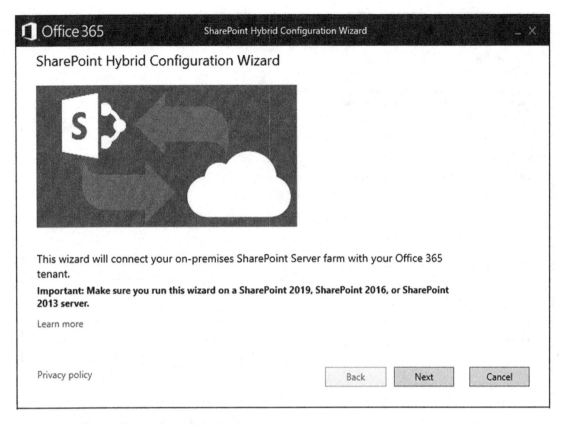

Figure 7-2. SharePoint Hybrid Configuration Wizard

7. To set up a hybrid environment for SharePoint or OneDrive for Business (OD4B), you must provide administrator credentials for both SharePoint Server and Office 365.

8. Click **Next** (Figure 7-3).

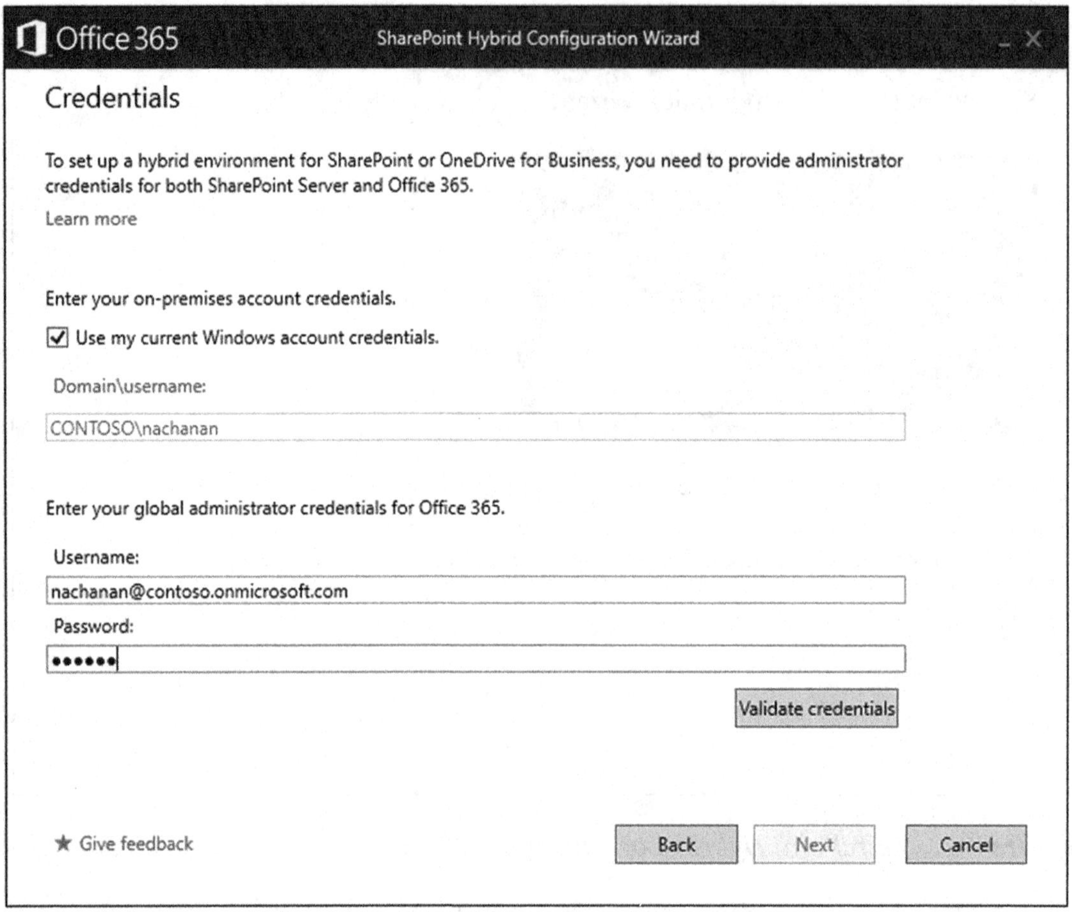

Figure 7-3. *Providing administrator credentials*

9. A prerequisites check report will be generated (Figure 7-4).

Figure 7-4. Hybrid configuration prerequisites check

SPO365LinkSettings Overview

SharePoint O365 Link Settings need to be set for the hybrid configuration. If you have not set them already, the prerequisites report will report it. The Set-SPO365LinkSettings cmdlet will help you configure hybrid features (such as hybrid site redirection, OneDrive redirection, ODB default to the cloud).

1. Open the **SharePoint 2019 Management Shell** with administrator privileges.

2. Run the following command (also shown in Figure 7-5):

   ```
   Set-SPO365LinkSettings -MySiteHostUrl "http://mysites.
   contoso.com" -RedirectSites $true
   ```

Figure 7-5. *Configuring the SharePoint O365 Link Settings*

Rerunning the SharePoint Hybrid Configuration Wizard

1. Rerun the prerequisites check report to see that all prerequisites are met. Click **Next** (Figure 7-6).

Figure 7-6. *Hybrid configuration prerequisites check*

2. Select the features to use in a hybrid environment. Click **Next** (Figure 7-7).

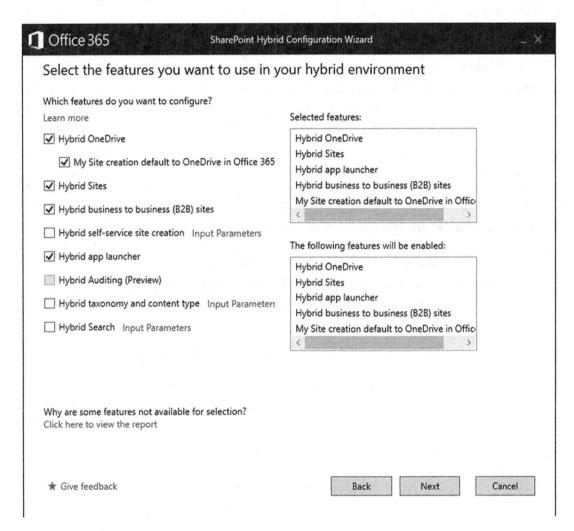

Figure 7-7. Hybrid configuration prerequisites check

3. The SharePoint Hybrid Configuration Wizard will run (Figure 7-8).

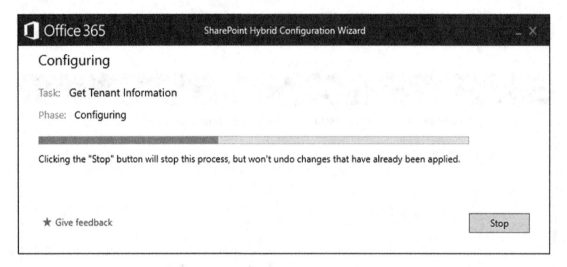

Figure 7-8. *SharePoint Hybrid Configuration Wizard*

4. After the successful run of the configuration wizard, the
   SharePoint server environment will be connected to Office 365.
   The summary report will be generated. Click **Close** (Figure 7-9).

Figure 7-9. *Hybrid configuration summary*

5. Perform **IISReset** on SharePoint Server 2019.

Configuration Summary

By default, the following features are configured to use in a hybrid environment.

Hybrid OneDrive: All SharePoint users will be redirected to OneDrive in Office 365. If you want only specific users to be redirected, follow this process.

1. Open **SharePoint Server 2019 Central Administration**.

2. From the left menu, click **Office 365**.

3. Under **Office 365**, click **Configure hybrid OneDrive and Sites features** (Figure 7-10).

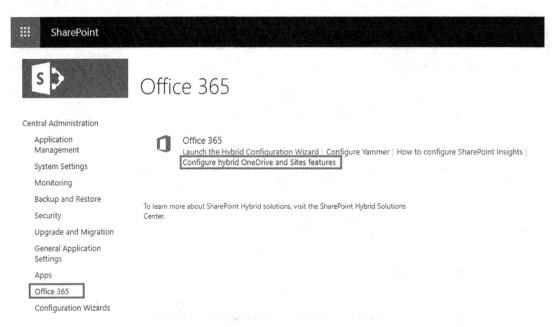

Figure 7-10. *Office 365 menu in SharePoint Server 2019 central administration*

4.   Specify specific audiences to use hybrid features.

5.   Click **OK** (Figure 7-11).

Configure hybrid OneDrive and Sites features

Use the hybrid settings on this page to integrate SharePoint
Server 2016 with Office 365 OneDrive and Sites.

Configure hybrid OneDrive and Sites features

To manually configure hybrid OneDrive and Sites features,
check the prerequisites and use the settings below

Use the Hybrid Picker to automatically configure hybrid
OneDrive and Sites features.   Learn more

My Site URL

To find your My Site URL, sign in to Office 365 as the Office
365 global admin.

My Site URL:

[https://tspfo365-my.sharepoint.com/]   (Try link)

Select audience for hybrid features

If you want only a specific set of users to use hybrid
features, you can select an existing audience or create a new
audience.

◉ Everyone

○ Use a specific audience:

[   ]   🔍 📇

Select hybrid features

◉ OneDrive and Sites
   Redirect OneDrive for Business to OneDrive on Office 365 and turn on hybrid Sites features. Learn more

○ OneDrive only
   Redirect OneDrive for Business to OneDrive on Office 365 so users can save and share documents from any device. No other SharePoint on-
   premises features are affected. Learn more

○ None
   Turn off hybrid OneDrive and Sites features.

Figure 7-11. *Configuring hybrid OneDrive and Site features*

Testing the Hybrid Environment

After configuring the hybrid environment, you can test the following features:

- **My Site creation default to OneDrive in Office 365:** My site creation experience for end users will be redirected to the Office 365 OneDrive experience. OneDrive will default to the cloud.

- **Hybrid business-to-business (B2B) sites:** You can now navigate across intranet sites in on-premises and extranet sites in SharePoint Online by using the Follow gesture on site pages. A new hybrid B2B extranet site can be created from the SharePoint Online Admin Center by clicking New on the site collections page. This site can later be shared with external users.

- **Hybrid app launcher:** Not all SharePoint Server users will have the hybrid app launcher. It can be restricted to specific target audiences from SharePoint 2019 Central Administration ➤ Office 365 ➤ Configure hybrid OneDrive and Sites features. The app launcher will now allow users to start using Office 365 features. So when a user selects OneDrive from the app launcher, they will be redirected to OneDrive for Business in Office 365. Similarly, when a user selects SharePoint from the app launcher, they will be redirected to the SharePoint Online (Figure 7-12).

Figure 7-12. *Hybrid app launcher*

Conclusion

The hybrid SharePoint Server experience brings together the best SharePoint on-premises and SharePoint Online (the cloud) features. The hybrid SharePoint Server environment enables trusted communication between SharePoint on-premises and SharePoint Online.

In the next chapter, you will explore how to register the public domain with Office 365 instead of using the default provided domain.

CHAPTER 8

Registering a Public Domain with Office 365

Office 365 comprises various software as services including the Office suite, SharePoint, Dynamics 365, Teams, Flow, OneNote, OneDrive, and Planner. Office 365 Education is free for schools and students with a valid school email address. Office 365 is widely used for collaboration across various organizations.

In this chapter, you will explore how to register a public domain with Office 365 instead of using the default provided domain.

Need for a Public Domain

When you sign up for Office 365, it provides a default domain in the format of xxx. onmicrosoft.com (where xxx is your tenant name chosen while setting up Office 365). The default domain works fine with no issues. However, if you are planning to set up Office 365 for a large organization, you're going to want a custom domain representing the organization. There are a variety of domain providers. The public domain then can be registered with Office 365 to point to that URL. There are a couple of ways to add the public domain to Office 365:

1. Buy a new domain and register it with Office 365.

2. Use an existing domain and register it with Office 365.

Buying a New Domain

If you do not have a domain already, buying a new domain from Office 365 might be a good option.

© Nanddeep Sadanand Nachan and Smita Sadanand Nachan 2020
N. S. Nachan and S. S. Nachan, *Understanding Hybrid Environments in SharePoint 2019*,
https://doi.org/10.1007/978-1-4842-6050-0_8

1. Open **Microsoft 365 Admin Center**.

2. Under **Settings**, click **Domains** (Figure 8-1).

Figure 8-1. *Domain options page*

3. Click **Buy domain**.

4. Find your new domain name by checking the availability. Click
    Next (Figure 8-2).

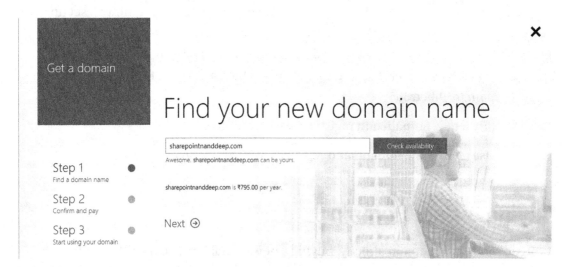

Figure 8-2. *Finding a new domain name*

5. Add the domain contact information.

6. Click **Next** (Figure 8-3).

Figure 8-3. *Specifying domain contact information*

7. Confirm your details and make a payment (Figure 8-4).

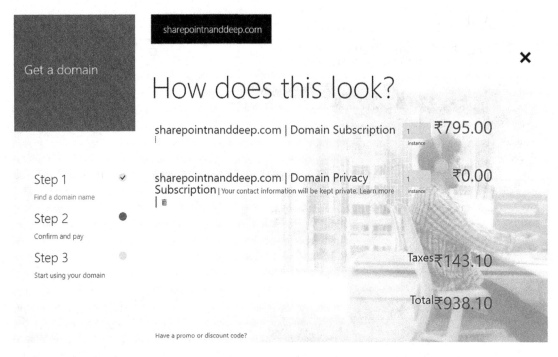

Figure 8-4. *Domain payment details*

8. After successful payment, click **Accept** in the dialog box to let Office 365 make domain entries in the GoDaddy domain center.

Using an Existing Domain

If you already have a public domain, it can be configured in Office 365 for use.

1. Open **Microsoft 365 Admin Center**.

2. Under **Settings**, click **Domains**.

3. Click **Add domain**.

4. In the dialog box, enter the domain name you own.

5. Click **Use this domain** (Figure 8-5).

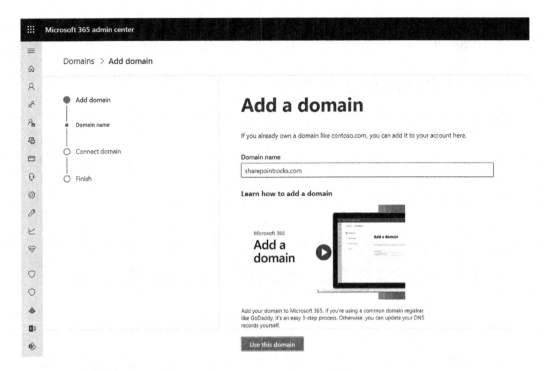

Figure 8-5. *Adding a domain*

6. Activate all services for your domain, like email and instant messaging, by adding DNS records for the domain at your registrar or DNS hosting provider (Figure 8-6).

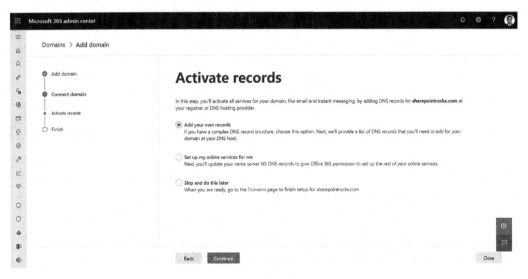

Figure 8-6. *Activating records*

7. Another option is to use **Add a TXT record** (Figure 8-7).

Add DNS records

To add these records for sharepointrocks.com, go to Your DNS host. ✎

The DNS records are grouped by the services that the DNS records support. We recommend copy and paste to avoid errors, but you can also download or print this information.

⤓ Download CSV file   ⤓ Download Zone file   🖶 Print

☐ Exchange and Exchange Online Protection

Advanced Options   ∧

☑ Microsoft Teams and Skype for Business

Online communication services like chat, conference calls, and video calls are provided by Microsoft Teams and Skype for Business. Teams and Skype need 4 records: 2 SRV records for user-to-user communication, and 2 CNAME records to sign-in and connect users to the service.

⌄ **CNAME Records (2)**
View instructions for CNAME Records

Record	Host Name	Points to address or value	TTL	Status
Expected	▢ sip	▢ sipdir.online.lync.com	▢ 1 Hour	
Expected	▢ lyncdiscover	▢ webdir.online.lync.com	▢ 1 Hour	

> **SRV Records (2)**

☑ Intune and Mobile Device Management for Office 365

This service helps you secure and remotely manage mobile devices that connect to your domain. Mobile Device Management needs 2 CNAME records so that users can enroll devices to the service.

⌄ **CNAME Records (2)**
View instructions for CNAME Records

Record	Host Name	Points to address or value	TTL	Status
Expected	▢ enterpriseregistration	▢ enterpriseregistration.windows.net	▢ 1 Hour	
Expected	▢ enterpriseenrollment	▢ enterpriseenrollment.manage.microsoft.com	▢ 1 Hour	

[Back] [Continue]   [Close]

Figure 8-7. *Adding DNS records*

8. Copy the values to your domain provider. (In my case, I am using BigRock as the domain provider; see Figure 8-8.)

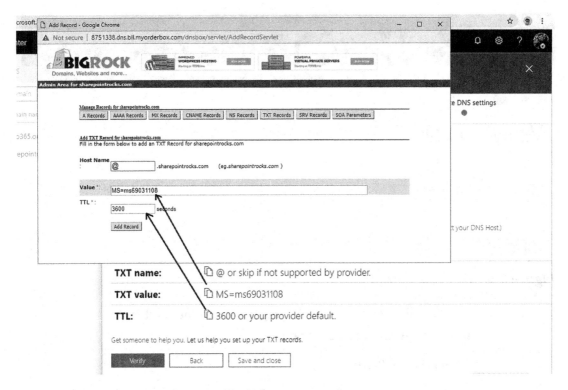

Figure 8-8. *Copying values to the domain provider*

9. Once the TXT record is added, navigate back to the Microsoft 365 Admin Center.

10. Click **Verify**. The domain will be verified.

11. Click **Next** (Figure 8-9).

Verify domain

Figure 8-9. *Verifying the domain*

12. Set up your online services by selecting the recommended option of **Set up my online services for me**.

13. Click **Next** (Figure 8-10).

Set up your online services

To set up your online services, you'll need to add one or more DNS records to your host.
What are DNS records?

◉ **Set up my online services for me. (Recommended)**
Next, you'll update your name server DNS records to give Office 365 permission to set up the rest of your online services.

○ **I'll manage my own DNS records.**
We will provide a list of DNS records that you will need to add for your domain at your DNS hosting provider.

| Next | Back | Save and close |

Figure 8-10. *Setting up online services*

14. Choose some online services.

15. Click **Next** (Figure 8-11).

Figure 8-11. *Choosing online services*

16. Click **Import DNS records**. Office 365 will query your site's existing DNS records and automatically import them.

17. Click **Next** (Figure 8-12).

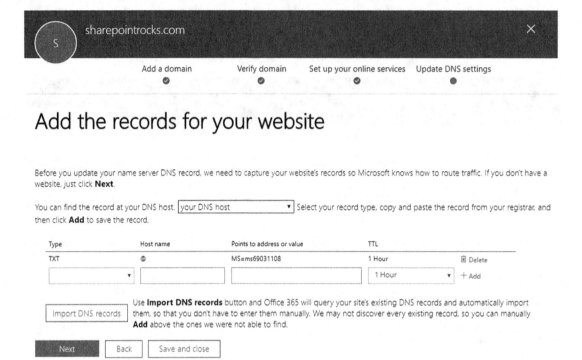

Figure 8-12. *Adding the records to website*

18. Activate the services for your domain, like email and instant messaging, by adding DNS records for your domain at your registrar or DNS hosting provider.

19. Click **Verify** (Figure 8-13).

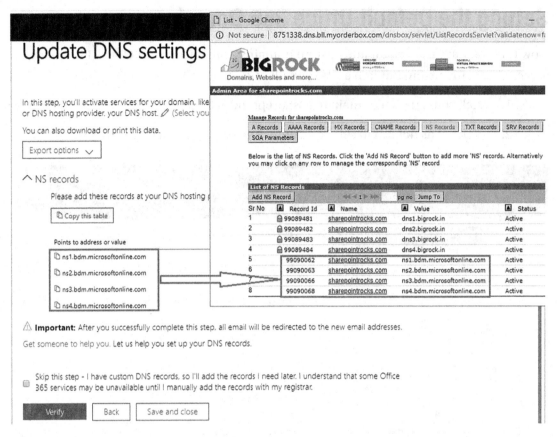

Figure 8-13. *Updating DNS settings*

20. The domain should appear under the Office 365 portal (Figure 8-14).

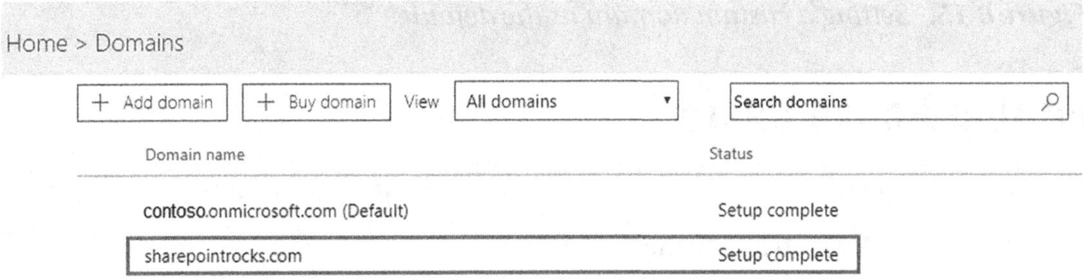

Figure 8-14. *The domain under the Office 365 portal*

Setting the Default Office 365 Domain

Now that you have the default and custom domains available in your Office 365 tenant, you can set your custom domain as the default one.

1. Click your custom domain (e.g. sharepointrocks.com)

2. Click **Set as default** to set the custom domain as default (Figure 8-15).

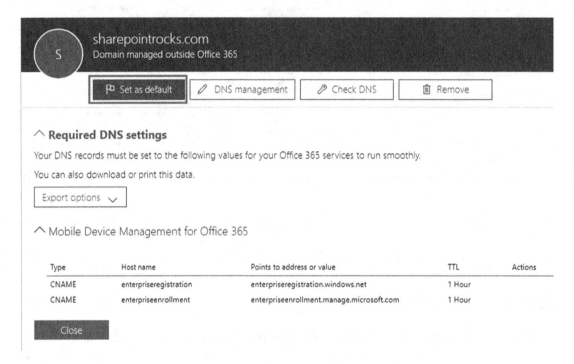

Figure 8-15. *Setting a custom domain as the default*

Editing Active Users

Now you must update the emails of active users to use your custom domain.

1. Open **Microsoft 365 Center**.

2. Under **Users**, click **Active Users**.

3. Select any user.

4. Click **Manage username** (Figure 8-16).

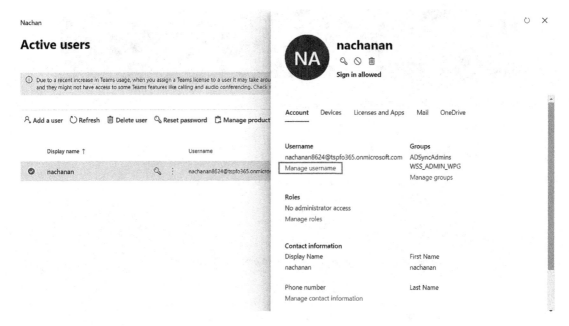

Figure 8-16. *Editing active users*

5.   Enter the new domain alias and set it as primary (Figure 8-17).

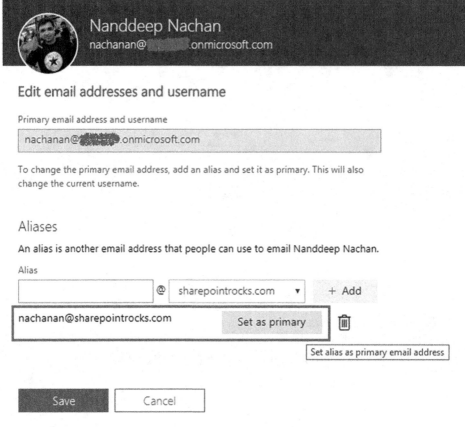

Figure 8-17. Setting a new domain alias as the primary

6.   Click **Save**.

7.   Sign out of the Office 365 portal and sign in with your new email
     address (Figure 8-18).

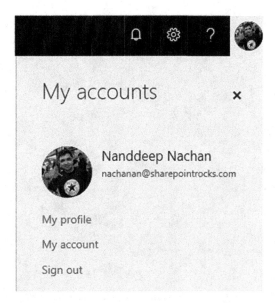

Figure 8-18. *Signing in with the new domain address*

Conclusion

Office 365 when set up provides a default domain (xxx.onmicrosoft.com). This public domain then can be registered with Office 365 so that Office 365 points to it. Or you may buy a new domain or use an existing domain.

In the next chapter, you will explore how to configure the underlying infrastructure to create a hybrid environment with SharePoint Server and Office 365.

CHAPTER 9

Configuring Office 365 for Hybrid SharePoint

When setting up the hybrid scenario, you must plan out certain steps on the SharePoint server and Office 365. Setting up a common UPN between these two environments is the crucial first step. In this chapter, you will explore how to configure the underlying infrastructure to create a hybrid environment with SharePoint Server and Office 365.

Prerequisites

It is important to have an Office 365 subscription and registered public domain so that you can set up a matching UPN (user profile name). It will help to synchronize the local active directory with Office 365.

1. Sign up for Office 365.

2. Get a public domain (from Office 365-supported vendors like GoDaddy.com or any third-party vendor).

3. Register the public domain with Office 365.

Adding a UPN suffix to the Local AD

The basic requirement is that the UPN configured in the local active directory must match the public domain name created and registered with Office 365. So, if the public domain registered with Office 365 is SharePointRocks.com, then the same should be used as a UPN suffix to be added to the local active directory.

© Nanddeep Sadanand Nachan and Smita Sadanand Nachan 2020
N. S. Nachan and S. S. Nachan, *Understanding Hybrid Environments in SharePoint 2019*,
https://doi.org/10.1007/978-1-4842-6050-0_9

Adding an Office 365-Registered UPN Suffix

As the first step, you need to add a UPN suffix that matches the public domain to the Local AD.

1. Open **Active Directory Domain and Trusts**.

2. Right-click the root node and click **Properties** (Figure 9-1).

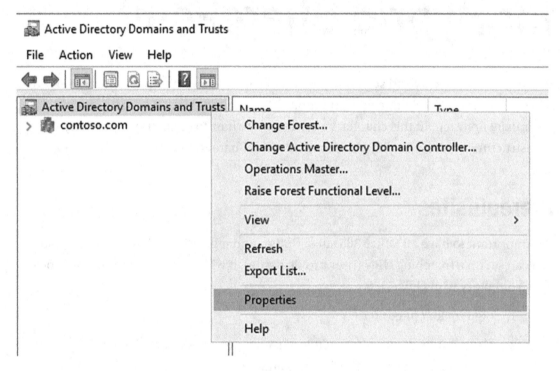

Figure 9-1. *Active Directory domains and trusts*

3. Add a Office 365-registered UPN suffix.

4. Click **OK** (Figure 9-2).

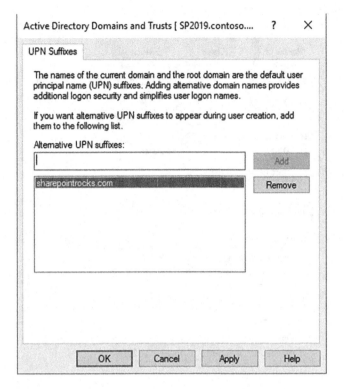

Figure 9-2. Adding a Office 365-registered UPN suffix

Updating a UPN for a Single User

Follow these steps to update a UPN for an individual user:

1. Open **Active Directory Users and Computers**.

2. Select any user to change the UPN.

3. Change the existing local domain to the new UPN.

4. Click **OK** (Figure 9-3).

Figure 9-3. *Active Directory user properties*

Managing Office 365 Directory from Azure Active Directory

You must synchronize the on-premises local active directory with the Office 365 directory. To do so, you enable the management of the Office 365 directory from Azure.

1. Open the **MS Azure portal** (https://portal.azure.com).

2. Click **Azure Active Directory ➤ Azure AD Connect**.

3. Click **Download Azure AD Connect** (Figure 9-4).

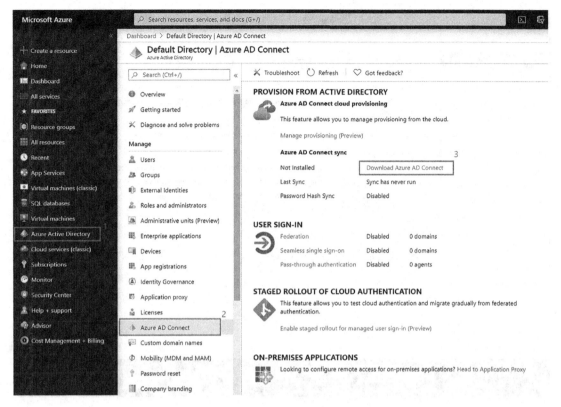

Figure 9-4. *Connecting to Azure Active Directory*

4. This will navigate to the **Microsoft Downloads Center**.

5. Download **Microsoft Azure Active Directory Connect**.

6. Double-click the downloaded file to install it.

7. Check the **I agree to the license terms and privacy notice** box.

8. Click **Continue** (Figure 9-5).

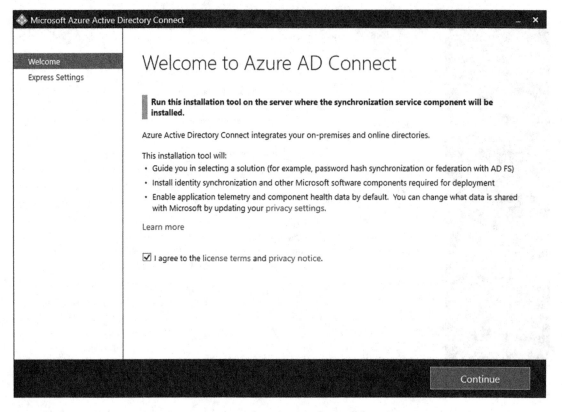

Figure 9-5. *Microsoft Azure Active directory connect*

9.   Click **Use express settings** to configure the identities of the local AD and synchronize.

10.   For more configuration options, click **Customize** (Figure 9-6).

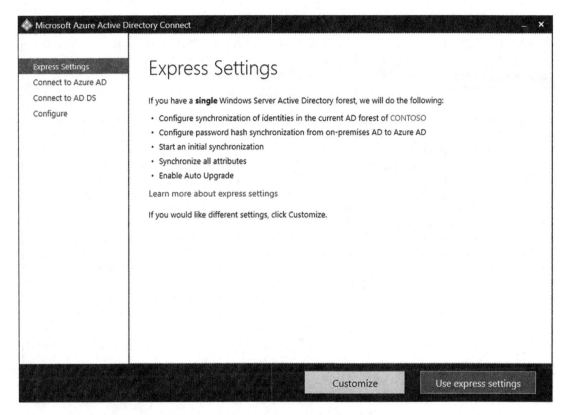

Figure 9-6. *MS Azure AD connect express settings*

11.   Specify Office 365 administrator credentials.

12.   Click **Next** (Figure 9-7).

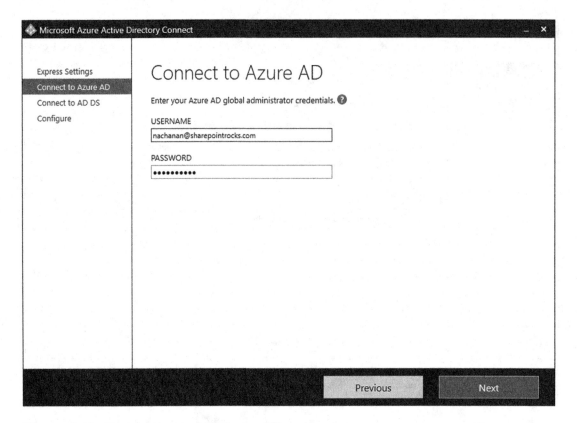

Figure 9-7. *Connecting to MS Azure AD*

13. Enter the Active Directory Domain Services enterprise
    administrator credentials.

14. Click **Next** (Figure 9-8).

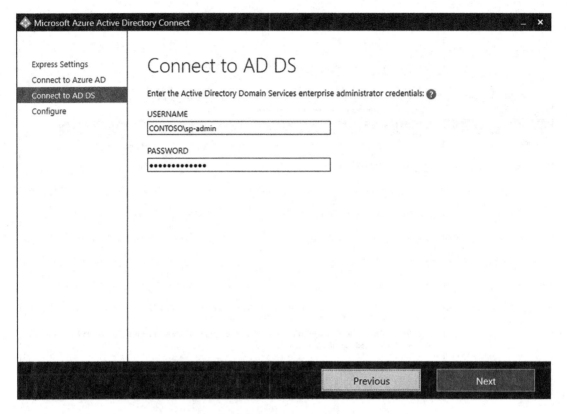

Figure 9-8. *Connecting to AD DS*

15. Select the **Continue matching all UPN suffixes to verified domains** checkbox.

16. Click **Next** (Figure 9-9).

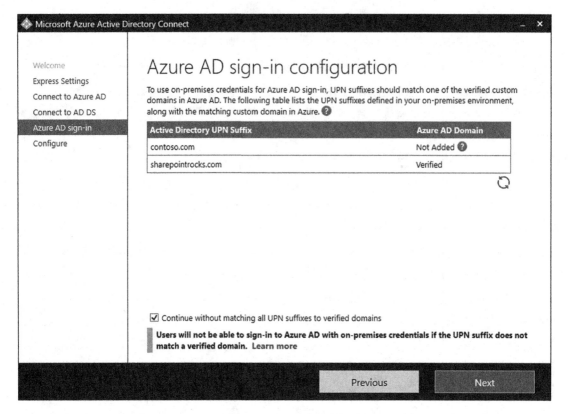

Figure 9-9.   *Azure AD sign-in configuration*

17.   The wizard is now ready to configure. It will install the synchronization engine, configure the Azure AD connector for Office 365, configure the local AD connector, enable password synchronization, enable auto upgrades, and configure synchronization services on the installed machine (Figure 9-10).

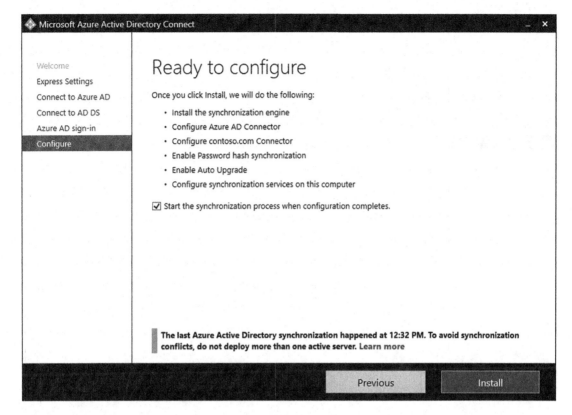

Figure 9-10. *Configuring Azure AD for the synchronization*

18.   The service configurations will take place. It will take some time to connect to both active directories and synchronize the users (Figure 9-11).

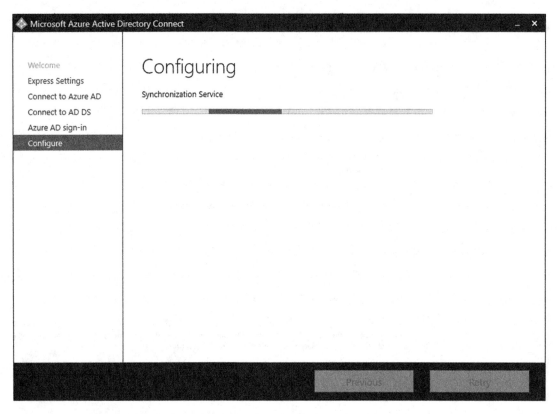

Figure 9-11. *Azure AD synchronization wizard*

19. Once the configuration is complete, check for any errors and warnings to fix.

20. Click **Exit** (Figure 9-12).

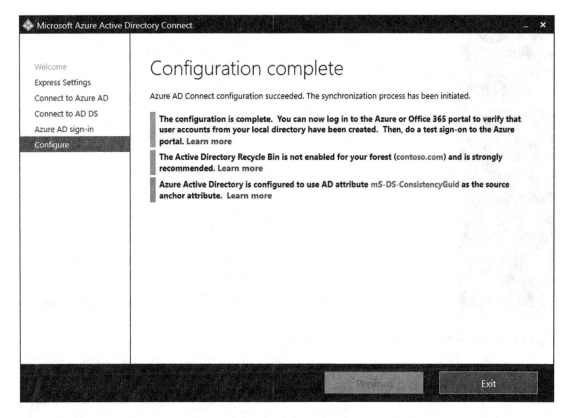

Figure 9-12. *Azure AD synchronization configuration completion*

Verifying User Sync

All users from the local AD should now be replicated to Office 365.

1. Open **Microsoft 365 Admin Center**.

2. In the left menu, under **Users**, click **Active users** (Figure 9-13).

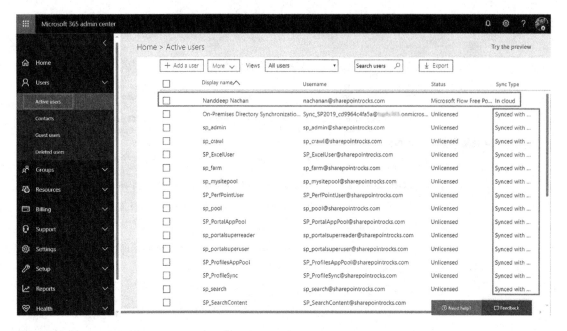

Figure 9-13. *Verifying user synchronization*

Assigning Licenses to Users

Once the accounts are synchronized, they should have a license in Office 365 to use hybrid features.

1.   Select the user to get a license.

2.   Select **Manage product licenses** (Figure 9-14).

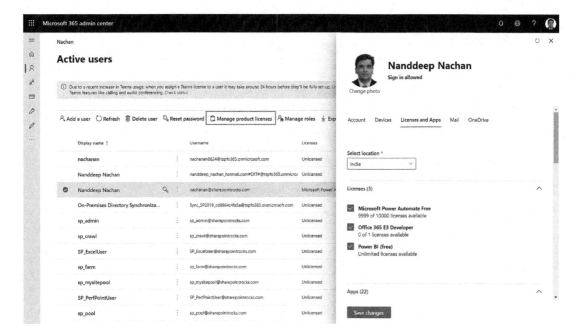

Figure 9-14. *Assigning licenses to users*

3. Select the location for the user. Turn on the required licenses for the user.

4. Click **Save changes**.

Conclusion

Setting up common UPNs between SharePoint Server and Office 365 environments is important to synchronize the users. This will help to set up a hybrid scenario.

In the next chapter, you will learn about self-service site creation and new feature offerings from SharePoint Server 2019 for the self-service site creation experience. You will set up a platform for understanding hybrid self-service site creation in the next chapter.

CHAPTER 10

SharePoint Server 2019 Self-Service Site Creation

Self-service site creation allows users with certain rights to create a site collection under a defined path. Like the preceding versions, SharePoint 2019 supports self-service site creation. However, SharePoint Server 2019 has gone beyond the normal self-service site creation and offers new features.

In this chapter, you will explore the concept of self-service site creation and new feature offerings from SharePoint Server 2019 for the self-service site creation experience. You will set up a platform for understanding hybrid self-service site creation during this next chapter.

Self-Service Site Creation

In a web application, there are two ways to create site collections.

- **Farm administrators:** Farm administrators can create a site collection using the SharePoint Central Administration site or from the SharePoint Management Shell (PowerShell). In this case, there is a dependency on farm administrators to create site collections. However, they can own the entire governance.

- **Self-service site creation:** Users with necessary permissions can create site collections under a defined path (e.g. /sites) within a particular web application. This option works well when you want a specific group of people to create site collections without waiting for the process.

© Nanddeep Sadanand Nachan and Smita Sadanand Nachan 2020
N. S. Nachan and S. S. Nachan, *Understanding Hybrid Environments in SharePoint 2019*,
https://doi.org/10.1007/978-1-4842-6050-0_10

What's New in SharePoint Server 2019?

SharePoint Server 2019 has the following offerings for self-service site creation:

- Self-service site creation in SharePoint 2019 allows you to create sites under different web applications. The web application can be from the same farm or on a remote farm.

- By default, it uses modern site templates for site creation. However, the classic site templates experience can be provided from the /_layouts/15/scsignup.aspx page.

- Farm administrators can control the Create Site link on the SharePoint home page.

Configuring Self-Service Site Creation

Follow these steps to configure self-service site creation.

1. Open **SharePoint 2019 Central Administration**.

2. Under **Application Management**, click **Manage web applications**.

3. Select the web application. Click **Self-Service Site Creation** from the ribbon (Figure 10-1).

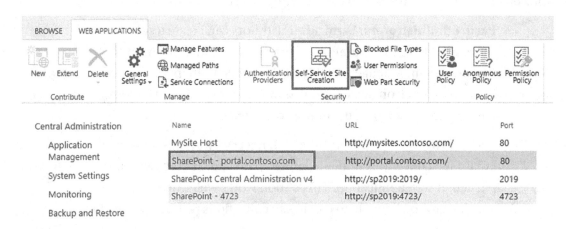

Figure 10-1. *Configuring self-service site creation*

4. The Self-Service Site Creation dialog will open (Figure 10-2).

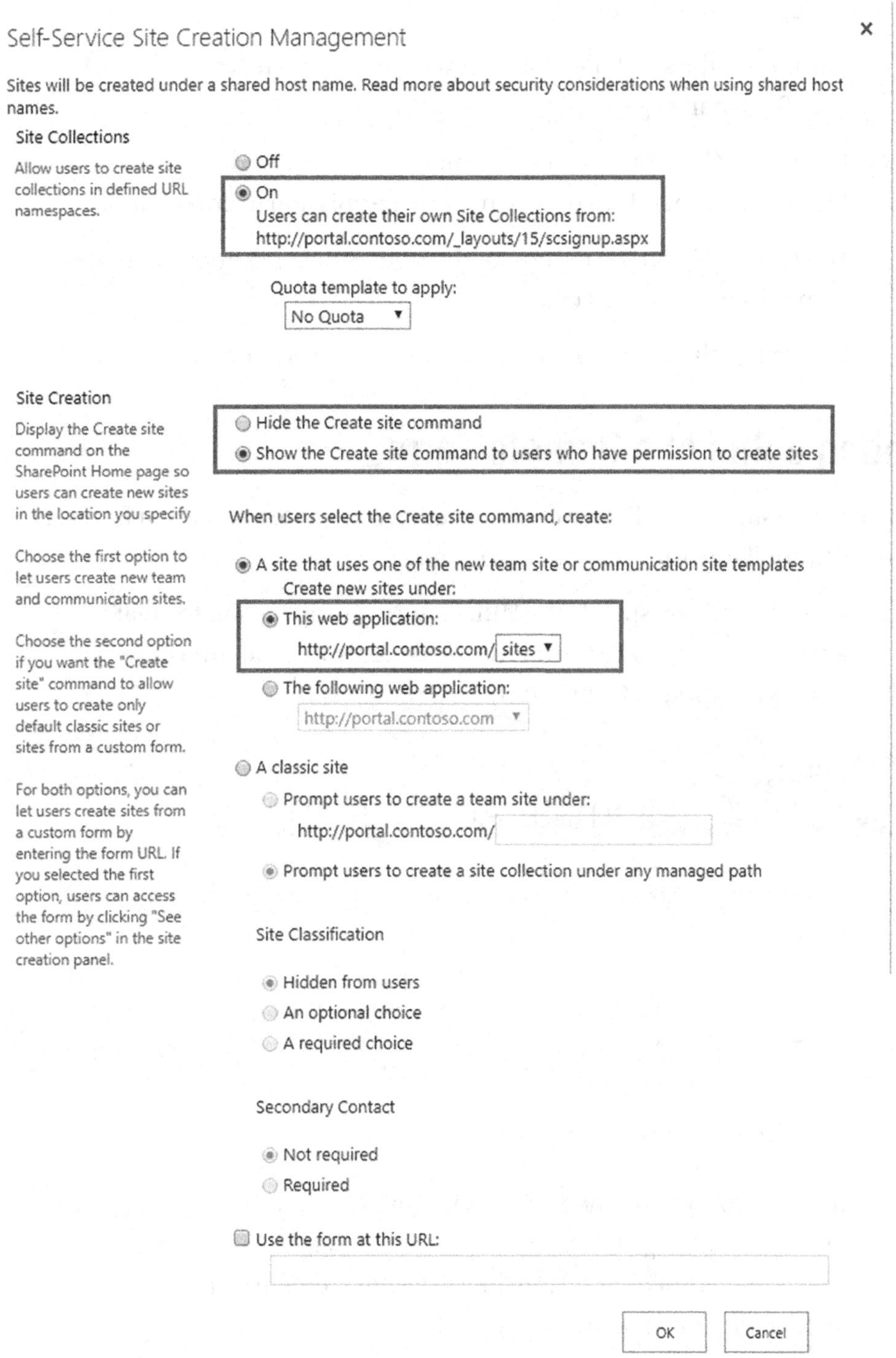

Self-Service Site Creation Management   ✕

Sites will be created under a shared host name. Read more about security considerations when using shared host names.

Site Collections

Allow users to create site collections in defined URL namespaces.

○ Off
◉ On
    Users can create their own Site Collections from:
    http://portal.contoso.com/_layouts/15/scsignup.aspx

    Quota template to apply:
    [No Quota ▼]

Site Creation

Display the Create site command on the SharePoint Home page so users can create new sites in the location you specify

Choose the first option to let users create new team and communication sites.

Choose the second option if you want the "Create site" command to allow users to create only default classic sites or sites from a custom form.

For both options, you can let users create sites from a custom form by entering the form URL. If you selected the first option, users can access the form by clicking "See other options" in the site creation panel.

○ Hide the Create site command
◉ Show the Create site command to users who have permission to create sites

When users select the Create site command, create:

◉ A site that uses one of the new team site or communication site templates
    Create new sites under:
    ◉ This web application:
        http://portal.contoso.com/[sites ▼]
    ○ The following web application:
        [http://portal.contoso.com ▼]

○ A classic site
    ○ Prompt users to create a team site under:
        http://portal.contoso.com/[   ]

    ◉ Prompt users to create a site collection under any managed path

Site Classification

◉ Hidden from users
○ An optional choice
○ A required choice

Secondary Contact

◉ Not required
○ Required

☐ Use the form at this URL:
[   ]

[OK]   [Cancel]

Figure 10-2. *Self-service site creation management*

In the dialog box, observe these options:

- Turning on the site collections allows users to create site collections in defined namespaces.

- Under Site Creation, the farm administrator can decide to show or hide site commands to users who have permission to create sites.

- You can decide on the current or different web applications and the managed path for site creation.

- Modern or classic site creation options can be selected from here.

Creating a Site in a Remote Farm

SharePoint 2019 supports self-service site creation in remote SharePoint farms. Follow these steps to configure site creation on a remote farm.

1. In the local farm, specify the URL of the web application to create a site in the **Map to External Resource** control in the **Alternate Access Mappings** (Figure 10-3).

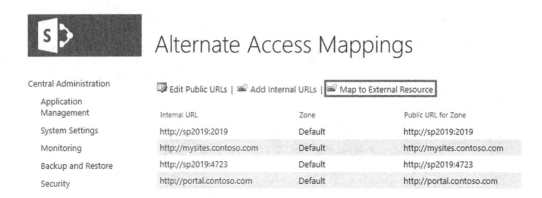

Figure 10-3. *Alternate access mappings*

2. In the local farm, on the **Self-Service Site Collection Management** page for the web application, select **The following web application** option, and then select the remote web application from the drop-down field.

3. In the remote farm, use the **Map to External Resource** control in the **Alternate Access Mappings** to specify the URL of the web application that hosts the SharePoint home page.

4. In the remote farm, enable self-service site creation for the web application on the **Self-Service Site Collection Management** page.

Conclusion

Self-service site creation is a good option when you want a specific group of people to create site collections without waiting for the process. SharePoint 2019 allows you to create sites under different web applications. The web application can be from the same farm or on a remote farm.

In the next chapter, you will explore the concept of hybrid self-service site creation and the various options available to enable the hybrid self-service site creation experience in SharePoint Server 2019.

CHAPTER 11

Hybrid Self-Service Site Creation

Hybrid self-service site creation was supported in previous versions of SharePoint on-premises (e.g. SharePoint Server 2013, 2016). The same experience is offered with SharePoint Server 2019. However, there are multiple options available in SharePoint Server 2019 to enable a hybrid self-service site creation experience. In this chapter, you will explore the concept of hybrid self-service site creation and the various options available to enable the hybrid self-service site creation experience in SharePoint Server 2019.

Hybrid Self-Service Site Creation

Hybrid self-service site creation redirects the default self-service site creation page in SharePoint Server to the SharePoint Online Group Creation page. This helps users create their sites in SharePoint Online instead of SharePoint Server on-premises. Hybrid self-service site creation follows the configured hybrid audience settings.

Enabling Hybrid Self-Service Site Creation via the SharePoint Hybrid Configuration Wizard

The SharePoint Hybrid Configuration Wizard supports the option to enable the hybrid self-service site creation experience. Follow these steps to enable a hybrid self-service site creation experience:

1. Open **SharePoint 2019 Central Administration**.

2. From the left navigation, click **Configuration Wizards**.

105

© Nanddeep Sadanand Nachan and Smita Sadanand Nachan 2020
N. S. Nachan and S. S. Nachan, *Understanding Hybrid Environments in SharePoint 2019*,
https://doi.org/10.1007/978-1-4842-6050-0_11

3. Under **Farm Configuration**, click **Launch the Hybrid Configuration Wizard** (Figure 11-1).

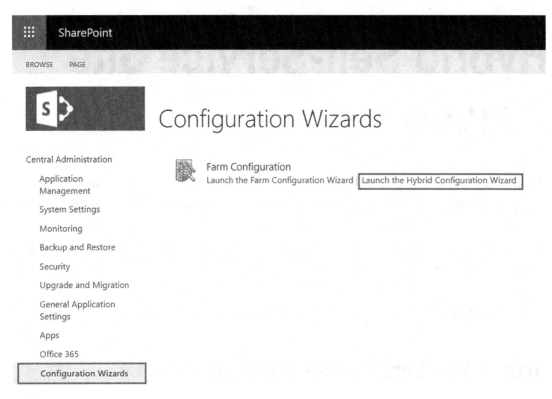

Figure 11-1. *Launching the Hybrid Configuration Wizard*

4. An executable file named HybridSPSetup.exe will be downloaded to the file system.

5. Double-click hybridspsetup.exe to run the SharePoint Hybrid Configuration Wizard.

6. On the **Select the features you want to use in your hybrid environment** page, select **Hybrid self-service site creation** (Figure 11-2).

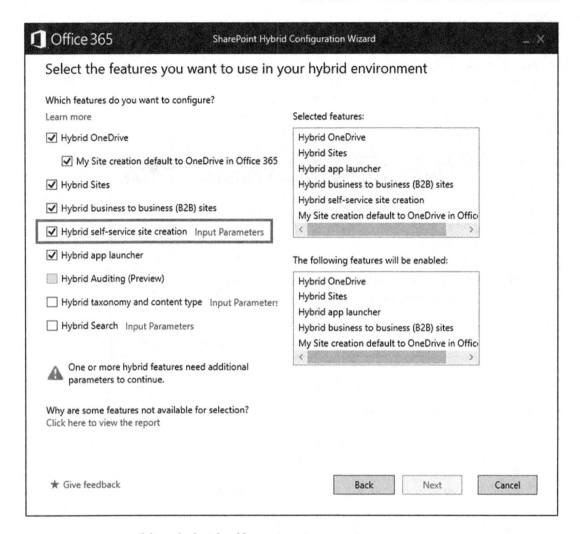

Figure 11-2. *Enabling hybrid self-service site creation*

7. Click **Input Parameters**, next to Hybrid self-service site creation.

8. Select the SharePoint Server 2019 on-premises web application (e.g. http://portal.contoso.com/) to use with hybrid self-service site creation.

9. Click **OK** (Figure 11-3).

Figure 11-3. *Selecting the web application to use with hybrid self-service site creation*

10. Click **Next** on the main wizard. The configuration will take place.

11. After successful configuration, self-service site creation for selected web applications will default to SharePoint Online.

12. Click **Close** (Figure 11-4).

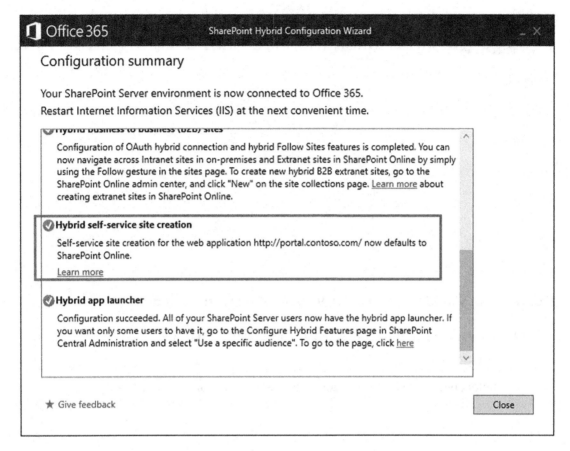

Figure 11-4. *SharePoint hybrid configuration summary*

13.   Perform **IISReset** on SharePoint Server 2019.

Managing Hybrid Self-Service Site Creation

Once the hybrid self-service site creation is configured, it can be managed from SharePoint 2019 Central Administration.

1.   Open **SharePoint 2019 Central Administration**.

2.   From the left menu, click **Application Management**.

3.   Under **Site Collections**, click **Configure self-service site creation** (Figure 11-5).

 Application Management

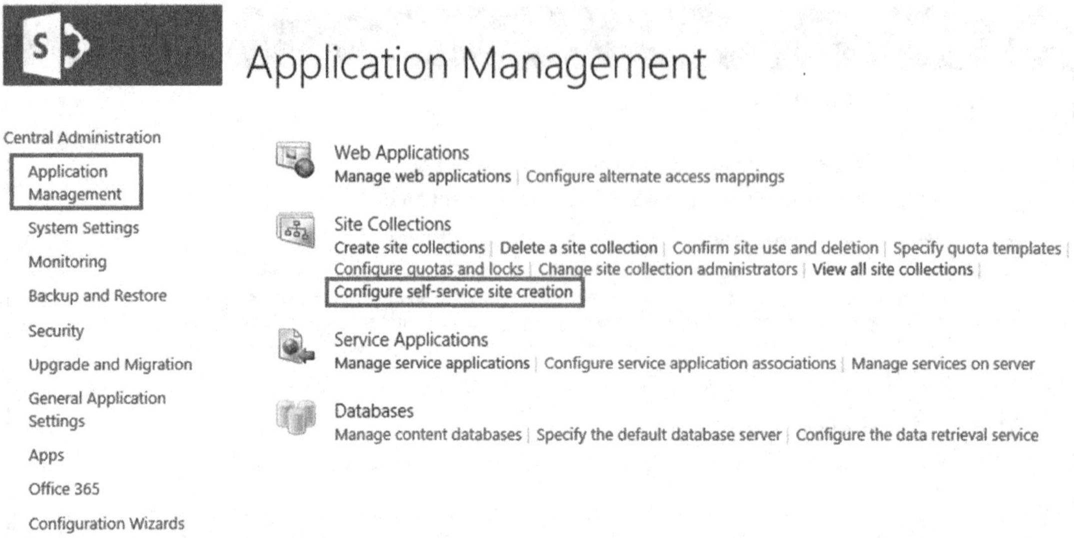

Central Administration

Application Management

System Settings

Monitoring

Backup and Restore

Security

Upgrade and Migration

General Application Settings

Apps

Office 365

Configuration Wizards

 Web Applications
Manage web applications | Configure alternate access mappings

 Site Collections
Create site collections | Delete a site collection | Confirm site use and deletion | Specify quota templates | Configure quotas and locks | Change site collection administrators | View all site collections |
Configure self-service site creation

 Service Applications
Manage service applications | Configure service application associations | Manage services on server

 Databases
Manage content databases | Specify the default database server | Configure the data retrieval service

Figure 11-5. *SharePoint Server 2019 application management*

4. Turn on the option for users to enable creating their site collections.

5. Select either classic or modern site creation options (Figure 11-6).

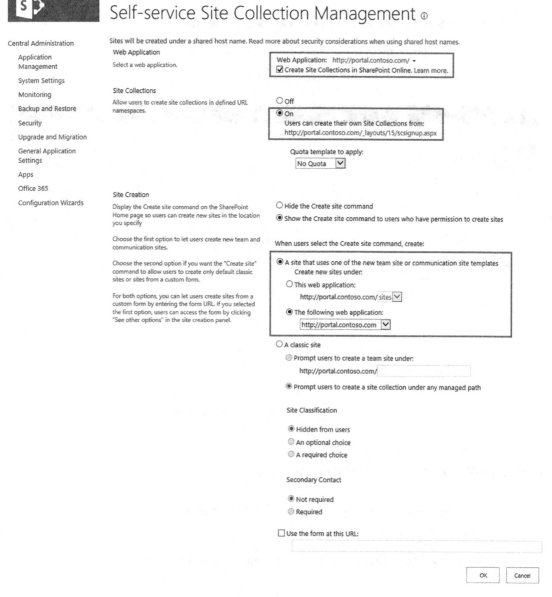

Figure 11-6. *Self-service site collection management*

The Create Site Collection Page

The Create Site Collection page in SharePoint 2019 provides an option to create a site collection in SharePoint Online.

1. Open **SharePoint 2019 Central Administration site**.

2. From the left menu, click **Application Management**.

3. Under **Site Collections**, click **Create site collections**.

4. The page lets users create this site collection in SharePoint Online. Click the **Click here** link (Figure 11-7).

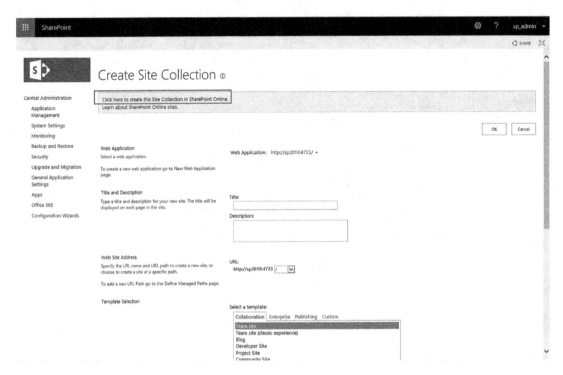

Figure 11-7. *The Create Site Collection page*

5. The login screen for SharePoint Online will appear. Enter the Office 365 administrator credentials.

6. The New Site Collection screen will appear (Figure 11-8).

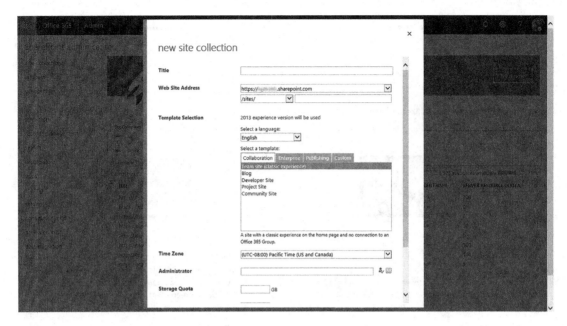

Figure 11-8. The New Site Collection screen

7.   Enter the required information to create a new site collection in SharePoint online.

Testing a Hybrid Self-Service Site Creation

The hybrid self-service site creation for the web application is configured at `http://portal.contoso.com/_layouts/15/scsignup.aspx`. Open the URL in the browser; it should navigate to the SharePoint Online site creation page (Figure 11-9).

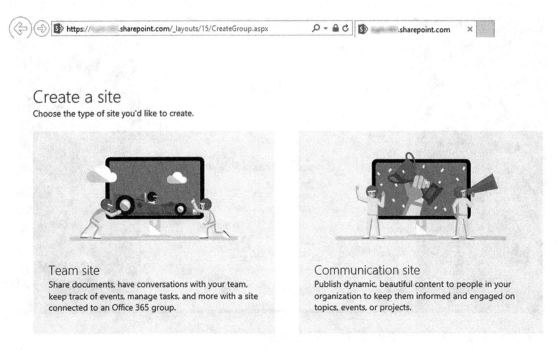

Figure 11-9. *Testing a hybrid self-service site creation*

Conclusion

Hybrid self-service site creation redirects the default self-service site creation page in SharePoint Server to the SharePoint Online Group Creation page. This helps users to create their sites in SharePoint Online instead of SharePoint Server on-premises.

In the next chapter, you will explore how to set up hybrid taxonomy. Also, you will configure synchronization between the cloud and on-premises taxonomy.

CHAPTER 12

Configuring a Hybrid Taxonomy with SharePoint Server 2019

Managed metadata is one of the useful service applications in SharePoint. Primarily it supports setting up a taxonomy for representing hierarchical business information. It also supports setting up a content type hub that centralizes the content types used across the sites.

In this chapter, you will learn how to set up a hybrid taxonomy. You will also configure synchronization between the cloud and the on-premises taxonomy.

SharePoint Hybrid Taxonomy

A SharePoint hybrid taxonomy helps to maintain a single taxonomy across SharePoint Server on-premises and SharePoint Online. You can choose the taxonomy groups to be shared between SharePoint Server on-premises and SharePoint Online. The shared taxonomy is maintained at SharePoint Online and a read-only copy is maintained at SharePoint Server on-premises.

SharePoint farm administrators can choose the taxonomy groups to replicate with SharePoint Online. The replicated taxonomy groups from SharePoint Online are available as read-only on SharePoint Server on-premises. SharePoint farm administrators can still modify the taxonomy groups, but the changes will get overwritten at the next hybrid synchronization.

© Nanddeep Sadanand Nachan and Smita Sadanand Nachan 2020
N. S. Nachan and S. S. Nachan, *Understanding Hybrid Environments in SharePoint 2019*,
https://doi.org/10.1007/978-1-4842-6050-0_12

Copying a SharePoint Server Taxonomy to SharePoint Online

To configure a hybrid taxonomy, you should first copy the existing taxonomy in SharePoint Server on-premises to SharePoint Online. You can select a set of taxonomy groups to start with. Later on, you may add more taxonomy groups as a part of the hybrid taxonomy by running the Hybrid Configuration Wizard.

Consider the example shown in Figure 12-1; this taxonomy exists in SharePoint Server on-premises.

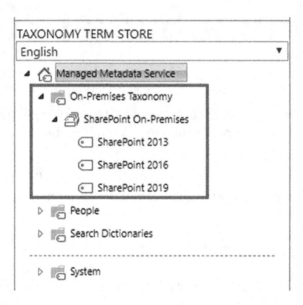

Figure 12-1. *SharePoint Server on-premises taxonomy term store*

Also, consider the taxonomy set up in SharePoint Online, shown in Figure 12-2.

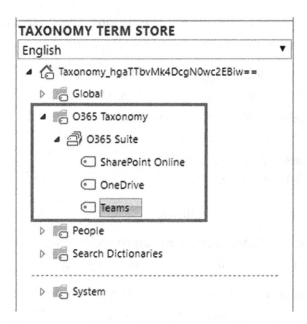

Figure 12-2. *SharePoint Online taxonomy term store*

Copying Taxonomy Groups

The **Copy-SPTaxonomyGroups** PowerShell cmdlet copies the taxonomy groups from SharePoint Server on-premises to SharePoint Online. This command also preserves user information (like owner, stakeholders, etc.) except active directory groups. You may replace the active directory group with actual users or with an Office 365 group.

1. Open **SharePoint 2019 Management Shell** with administrator privileges.

2. Run the following command to capture credentials to connect to SharePoint online:

```
$credential = Get-Credential
```

3. Run the following command to copy taxonomy groups from SharePoint Server on-premises to SharePoint Online:

```
Copy-SPTaxonomyGroups -LocalTermStoreName
"<ManagedMetadataServiceApplication>"
-LocalSiteUrl "<OnPremisesSiteURL>"
-RemoteSiteUrl "<SharePointOnlineSiteURL>"
-GroupNames "Group1","Group2"
-Credential $credential
```

The parameters specified are as follows:

- `LocalTermStoreName`: Name of managed metadata service application in SharePoint Server on-premises

- `LocalSiteURL`: URL of the SharePoint Server on-premises site where your taxonomy store is located

- `RemoteSiteURL`: URL of SharePoint Online site where term store is located (`https://<tenan>.sharepoint.com`)

- `GroupNames`: Taxonomy groups in SharePoint Server on-premises to be copied to SharePoint online

- `Credential`: Office 365 global administrator credentials

Example:

```
Copy-SPTaxonomyGroups -LocalTermStoreName "Managed Metadata Service"
-LocalSiteUrl "http://portal.contoso.com"
-RemoteSiteUrl "https://contoso.sharepoint.com"
-GroupNames "On-Premises Taxonomy"
-Credential $credential
```

Once the PowerShell cmdlet has run successfully, the SharePoint Server on-premises taxonomy groups will be copied to SharePoint Online (Figure 12-3).

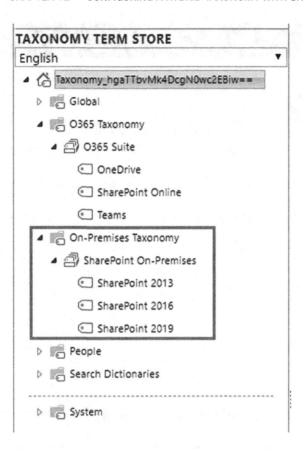

Figure 12-3. *SharePoint Server on-premises taxonomy groups copied to SharePoint Online*

Configuring a Hybrid SharePoint Taxonomy

The next step is to set up the hybrid connection, which will allow replication from SharePoint Online back to SharePoint Server on-premises. Follow these steps to download and run a hybrid picker tool.

1. Open the **SharePoint 2019 Central Administration** site.

2. From the left navigation, click **Configuration Wizards**.

3. Under Farm Configuration, click **Launch the Hybrid Configuration Wizard** (Figure 12-4).

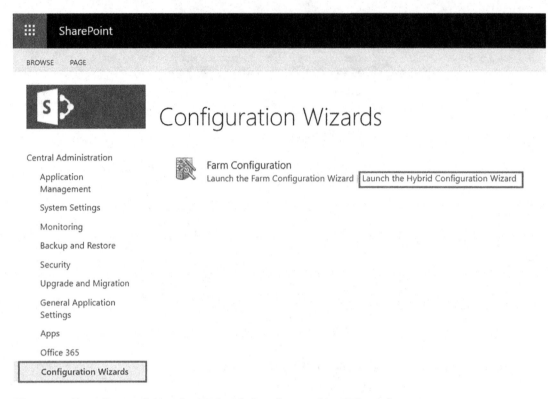

***Figure 12-4.** Launching the Hybrid Configuration Wizard*

4. An executable file named HybridSPSetup.exe will be downloaded to the file system.

5. Double-click HybridSPSetup.exe to install.

6. The wizard will open to connect your on-premises SharePoint Server farm with your Office 365 tenant.

7. Click **Next** (Figure 12-5).

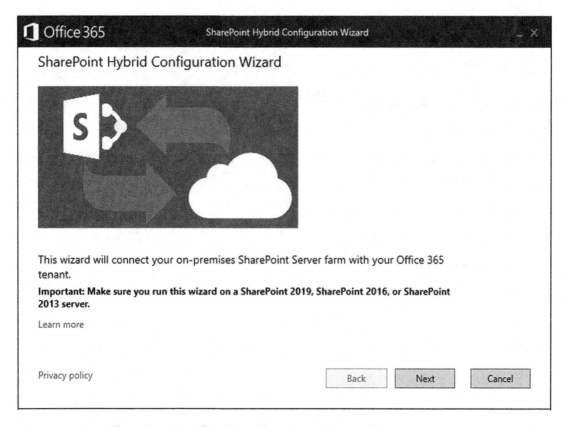

Figure 12-5. *SharePoint Hybrid Configuration Wizard*

8. To set up a hybrid environment for SharePoint or OneDrive for
    Business (OD4B), you need to provide administrator credentials
    for both SharePoint Server on-premises and Office 365.

9. Click **Next** (Figure 12-6).

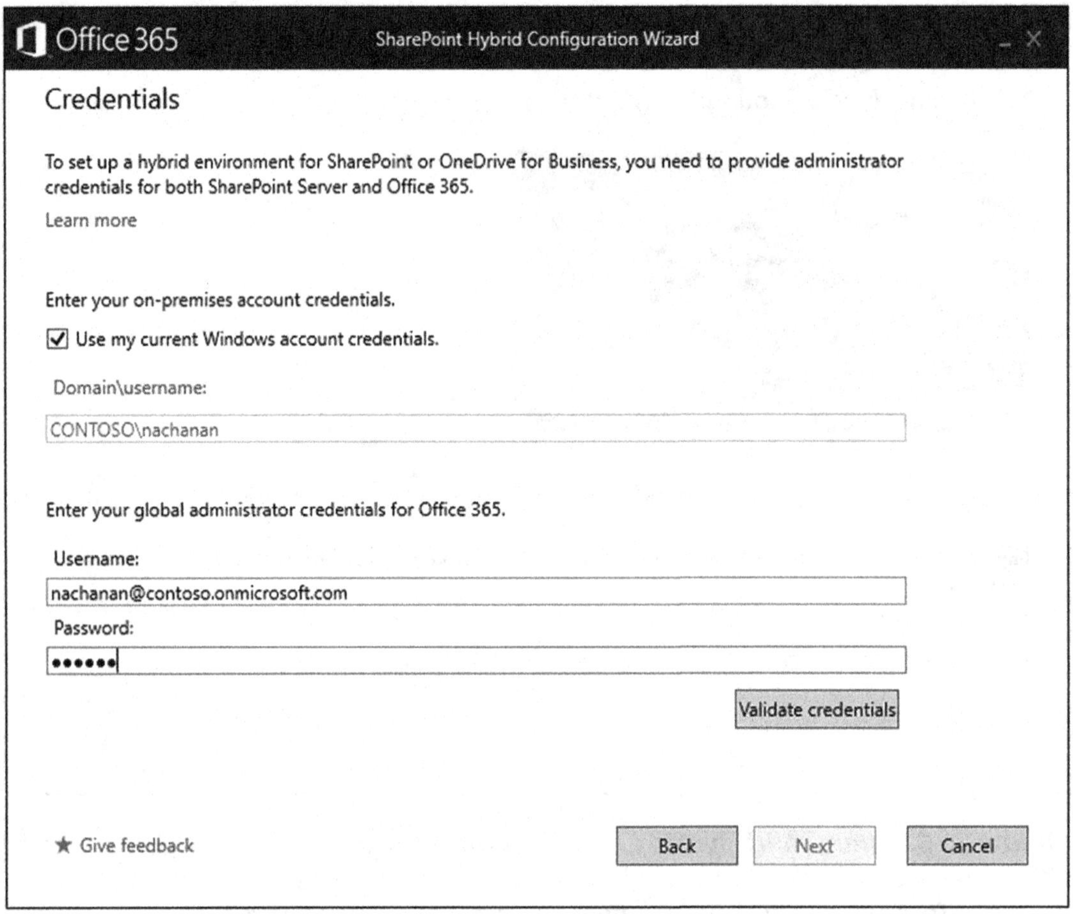

Figure 12-6. *Administrator credentials*

10. A prerequisites check report will be generated (Figure 12-7).

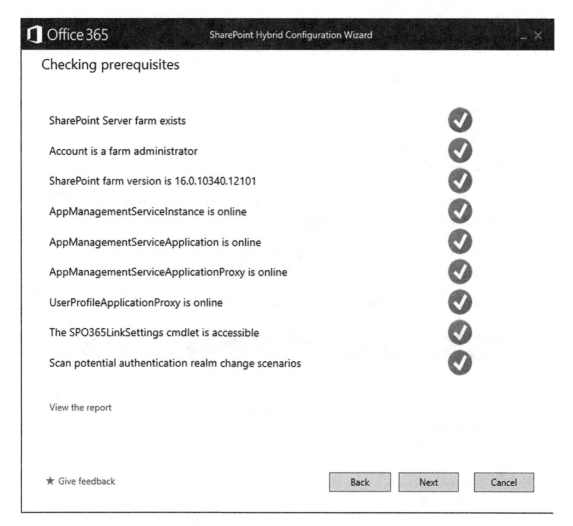

Figure 12-7. *Prerequisites check*

In case of any errors regarding the SPO365LinkSettings cmdlet, please follow these steps and rerun the SharePoint Hybrid Configuration Wizard:

- Open the **SharePoint 2019 Management Shell** with administrator privileges.

- Run the following command (also shown in Figure 12-8):

```
Set-SPO365LinkSettings -MySiteHostUrl "http://mysites.
contoso.com" -RedirectSites $true
```

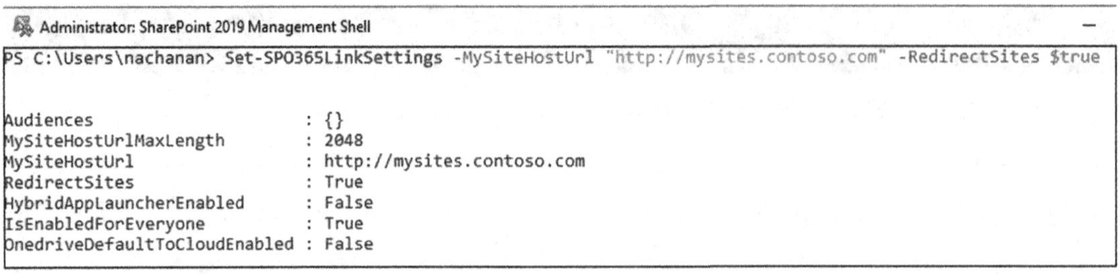

```
Administrator: SharePoint 2019 Management Shell                                              —

PS C:\Users\nachanan> Set-SPO365LinkSettings -MySiteHostUrl "http://mysites.contoso.com" -RedirectSites $true


Audiences                      : {}
MySiteHostUrlMaxLength         : 2048
MySiteHostUrl                  : http://mysites.contoso.com
RedirectSites                  : True
HybridAppLauncherEnabled       : False
IsEnabledForEveryone           : True
OnedriveDefaultToCloudEnabled  : False
```

Figure 12-8. *Set-SPO365LinkSettings*

11. Install the default features available in the Hybrid Environment Wizard. The configuration wizard will run.

12. After the successful run of the Hybrid Configuration Wizard, the SharePoint server environment will be connected to Office 365.

13. Select the **Hybrid taxonomy and content type** box (Figure 12-9).

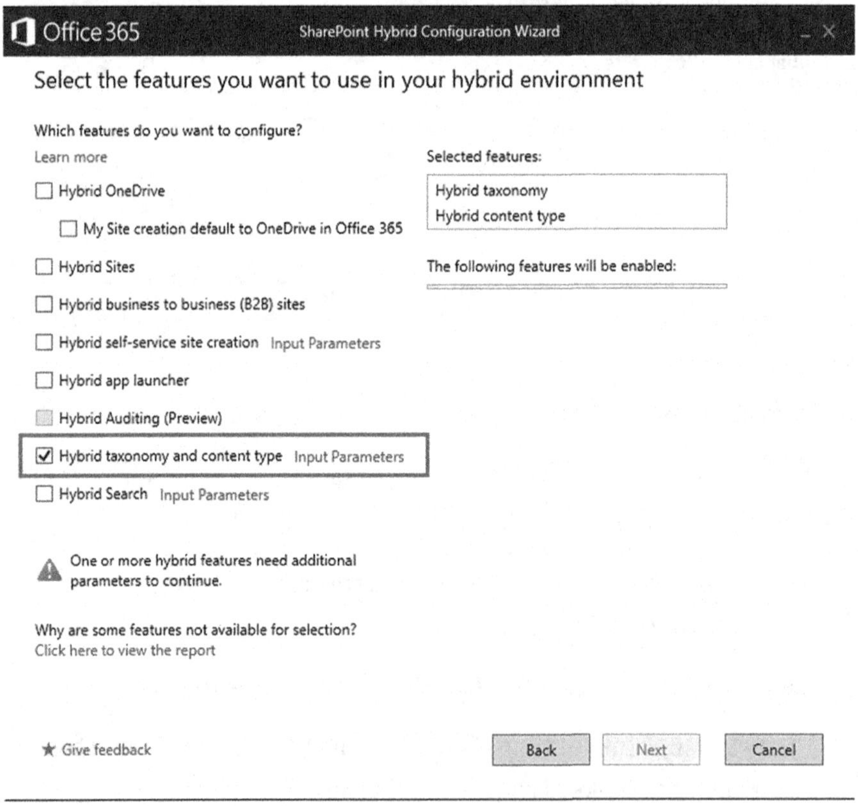

Figure 12-9. *Selecting the hybrid taxonomy and content type*

14.   Click the input parameters (Figure 12-10).

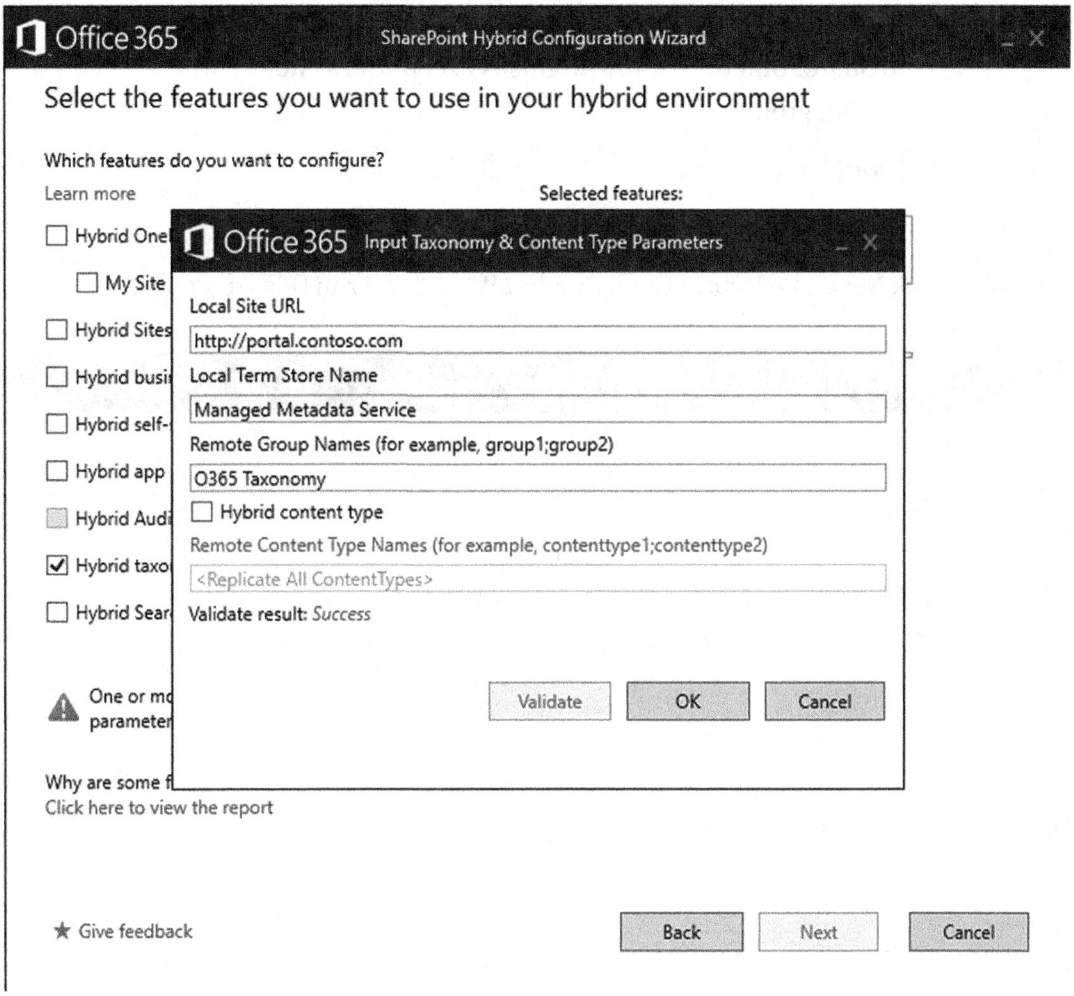

Figure 12-10. *Inputing taxonomy and content type parameters*

- In the **Local Site URL** field, specify the SharePoint server on-premises site URL.

- In the **Local Term Store Name** field, specify the SharePoint server on-premises managed service application name.

- In the **Remote Group Names** field, specify the SharePoint online taxonomy groups to be used for a hybrid. If kept blank, all the SharePoint online taxonomy groups will be replicated to SharePoint Server on-premises except the system and special groups.

15. Click **Validate**.

16. Once validation is successful, click **OK**.

17. Click **Next**. The Hybrid Configuration Wizard will run (Figure 12-11).

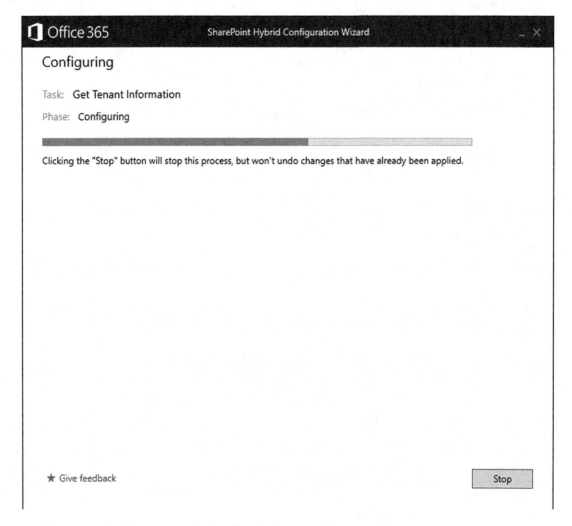

Figure 12-11. SharePoint Hybrid Configuration Wizard

18. Upon a successful run of the SharePoint Hybrid Configuration
     Wizard, the configuration summary will be shown (Figure 12-12).

Figure 12-12. Configuration summary

19. Click **Close**.

20. Perform **IISReset** on the SharePoint Server on-premises.

Timer Job

Now, return to SharePoint Server 2019 Central Administration. Open the Managed metadata service application and verify in the Taxonomy term store if the taxonomy groups from SharePoint Online have been replicated. Most may not be replicated, because hybrid taxonomy runs as a SharePoint timer job.

1. Open the **SharePoint Server 2019 Central Administration** site.

2. From the left menu, click **Monitoring**.

3. Under **Timer Jobs**, click **Check job status** (Figure 12-13).

Figure 12-13. *Checking job status*

4. From the left menu, click **Job Definitions**.

5. Find and select a timer job named **Taxonomy Groups Replication** (Figure 12-14).

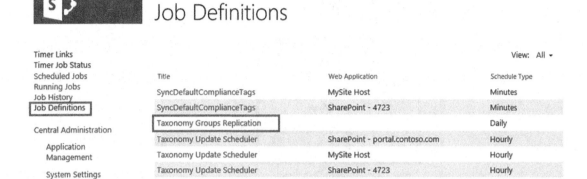

Title	Web Application	Schedule Type
SyncDefaultComplianceTags	MySite Host	Minutes
SyncDefaultComplianceTags	SharePoint - 4723	Minutes
Taxonomy Groups Replication		Daily
Taxonomy Update Scheduler	SharePoint - portal.contoso.com	Hourly
Taxonomy Update Scheduler	MySite Host	Hourly
Taxonomy Update Scheduler	SharePoint - 4723	Hourly

Figure 12-14. *Timer job named Taxonomy Groups Replication*

6. Run the timer job by clicking **Run Now**.

7. From the left menu, click **Running Jobs**. Wait for the timer job to finish running (Figure 12-15).

Figure 12-15. *Running jobs*

Verifying Taxonomy Groups Replication

From SharePoint 2019 Central Administration, navigate to the Managed Metadata Service application. Verify that the SharePoint Online taxonomy groups have been replicated (Figure 12-16).

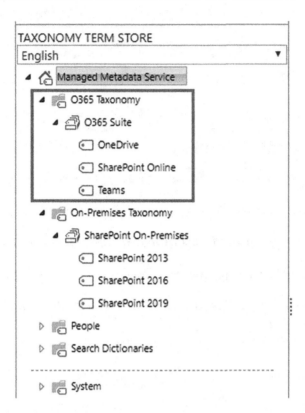

Figure 12-16. *Verifying taxonomy groups replication*

Conclusion

The SharePoint hybrid taxonomy helps to maintain a single taxonomy across SharePoint Server on-premises and SharePoint Online. The shared taxonomy is maintained at SharePoint Online and a read-only copy is maintained at SharePoint Server on-premises.

In the next chapter, you will explore how to set up hybrid content types. Also, you will configure synchronization between cloud and on-premises content types.

CHAPTER 13

Configuring Hybrid Content Types in SharePoint Server 2019

The Managed Metadata Service application in SharePoint is primarily used to set up a taxonomy for representing hierarchical business information. It also supports setting up a content type hub that centralizes the content types used across the sites.

In this chapter, you will explore how to set up hybrid content types. Also, you will configure synchronization between cloud and on-premises content types.

SharePoint Hybrid Content Types

SharePoint hybrid content types help to maintain a single set of content types across SharePoint Server on-premises and SharePoint Online. The shared content types are maintained at SharePoint Online and a read-only copy is maintained at SharePoint Server on-premises. The hybrid content types propagate the updates from SharePoint Online to SharePoint Server on-premises.

Content Type Hub in SharePoint Online

The content type hub in SharePoint Online is a predefined site collection. Follow these steps to locate your content type hub:

1. Open the **SharePoint Online** root site.

2. Navigate to **site settings**.

131

N. S. Nachan and S. S. Nachan, *Understanding Hybrid Environments in SharePoint 2019*,
https://doi.org/10.1007/978-1-4842-6050-0_13

3. Under **Site Collection Administration**, click **Content type publishing** (Figure 13-1).

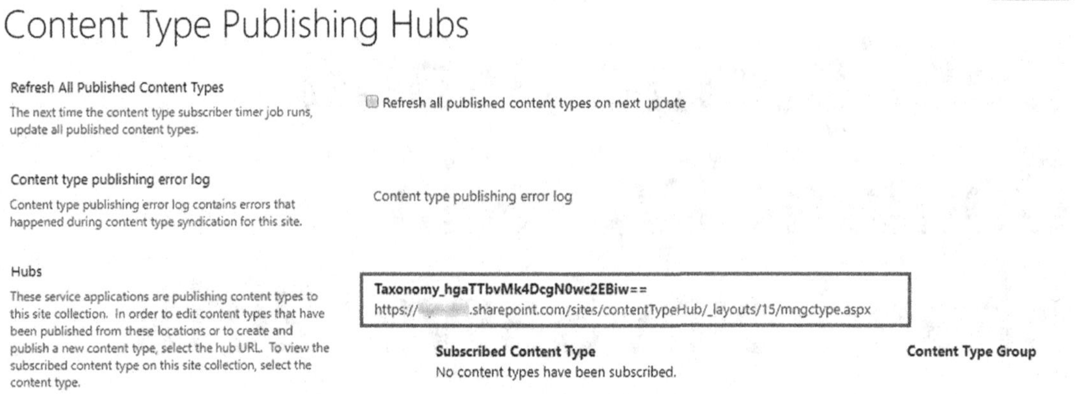

Content Type Publishing Hubs

Refresh All Published Content Types

The next time the content type subscriber timer job runs, update all published content types.

☐ Refresh all published content types on next update

Content type publishing error log

Content type publishing error log contains errors that happened during content type syndication for this site.

Content type publishing error log

Hubs

These service applications are publishing content types to this site collection. In order to edit content types that have been published from these locations or to create and publish a new content type, select the hub URL. To view the subscribed content type on this site collection, select the content type.

Taxonomy_hgaTTbvMk4DcgN0wc2EBiw==
https:// █████.sharepoint.com/sites/contentTypeHub/_layouts/15/mngctype.aspx

Subscribed Content Type   **Content Type Group**
No content types have been subscribed.

Figure 13-1. *Content type publishing hubs*

4. Under the **Hubs** section, the content type hub URL for the tenant is listed along with subscribed content types.

5. Click the hub URL to navigate to the Site Content Types page of the content type hub.

6. Create a new content type (Figure 13-2).

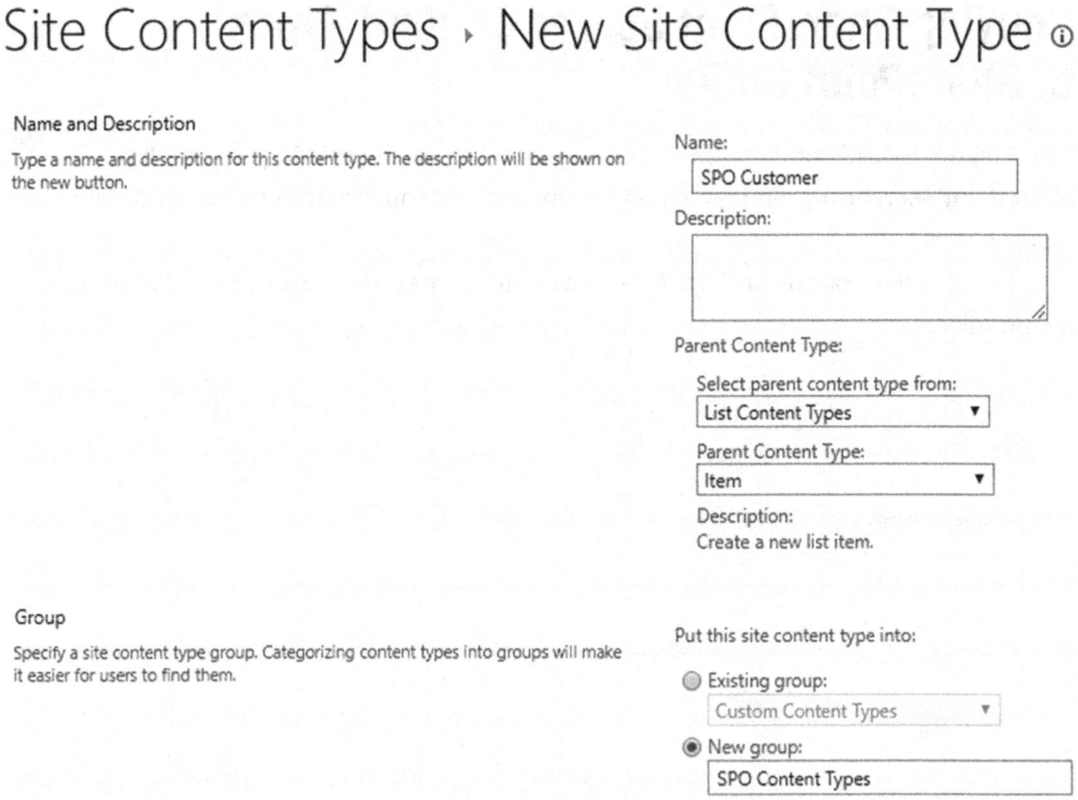

Site Content Types › New Site Content Type ⓘ

Name and Description

Type a name and description for this content type. The description will be shown on the new button.

Name:

SPO Customer

Description:

Parent Content Type:

Select parent content type from:

List Content Types ▾

Parent Content Type:

Item ▾

Description:
Create a new list item.

Group

Specify a site content type group. Categorizing content types into groups will make it easier for users to find them.

Put this site content type into:

○ Existing group:

Custom Content Types ▾

⦿ New group:

SPO Content Types

Figure 13-2. *Creating a new content type*

7.   Now add existing site columns to your content type (Figure 13-3).

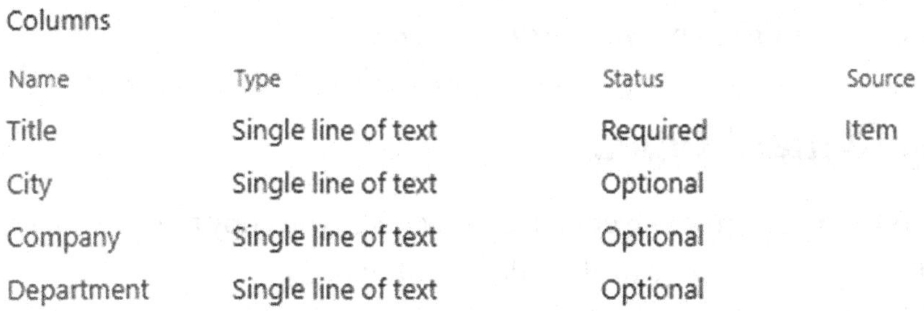

Name	Type	Status	Source
Columns			
Title	Single line of text	Required	Item
City	Single line of text	Optional	
Company	Single line of text	Optional	
Department	Single line of text	Optional	

Figure 13-3. *Adding existing site columns to a content type*

Copying SharePoint Server Content Types to SharePoint Online

To configure hybrid content types, you should first copy the existing content types in SharePoint Server on-premises to SharePoint Online. You can select a set of content types to start with.

Consider the example in Figure 13-4 of content types that exist in SharePoint Server on-premises.

Site Content Types · Site Content Type

Site Content Type Information

Name: SP OnPrem Vendor
Description:
Parent: Item
Group: SP OnPrem Content Types

Columns

Name	Type	Status	Source
Title	Single line of text	Required	Item
Office	Single line of text	Optional	
E-Mail	Single line of text	Optional	
Location	Single line of text	Optional	

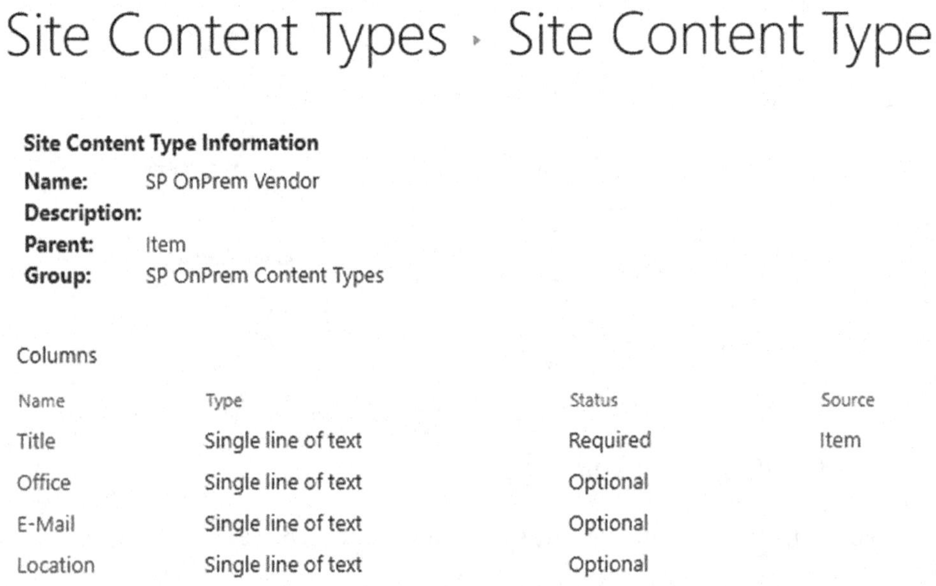

Figure 13-4. *Existing on-premises content types*

Copying Content Types

The **Copy-SPContentTypes** PowerShell cmdlet helps you copy the content types from SharePoint server on-premises to SharePoint Online.

1. Open the **SharePoint 2019 Management Shell** with administrator privileges.

2. Run the following command to capture the credentials to connect to SharePoint Online:

   ```
   $credential = Get-Credential
   ```

3. Run the following command to copy the content types from
    SharePoint Server on-premises to SharePoint Online:

```
Copy-SPContentTypes -LocalSiteUrl http://localsite/
-LocalTermStoreName "Managed Metadata Service Application "
-RemoteSiteUrl https://contoso.sharepoint.com/
-ContentTypeNames @("ContentTypeA", "ContentTypeB")
-Credential $credential
```

The parameters specified are as follows:

- LocalSiteUrl: URL of the SharePoint Server on-premises site where
  your taxonomy store is located

- LocalTermStoreName: Name of managed metadata service
  application in SharePoint Server on-premises

- RemoteSiteURL: URL of SharePoint Online site where the term store is
  located (https://<TenantName>.sharepoint.com)

- ContentTypeNames: Content types in SharePoint Server on-premises
  to be copied to SharePoint Online

- Credential: Office 365 global administrator credentials

Example:

```
Copy-SPContentTypes -LocalSiteUrl http://portal.contoso.com
-LocalTermStoreName "Managed Metadata Service Application"
-RemoteSiteUrl https://contoso.sharepoint.com
-ContentTypeNames @("SP OnPrem Vendor")
-Credential $credential
```

Once the PowerShell cmdlet runs successfully, the SharePoint Server on-premises
content types will be copied to SharePoint Online.

Configuring Hybrid SharePoint Content Types

The next step is to set up the hybrid connection, which will allow replication from
SharePoint online back to the SharePoint server on-premises. Follow these steps to
download and run a hybrid picker tool:

1. Open the **SharePoint 2019 Central Administration** site.

2. From the left navigation, click **Configuration Wizards**.

3. Under **Farm Configuration**, click **Launch the Hybrid Configuration Wizard** (Figure 13-5).

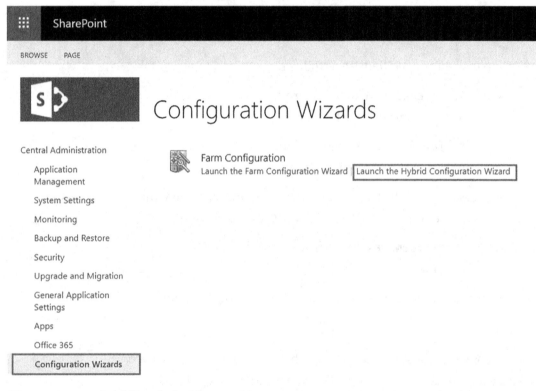

Figure 13-5. *Enabling hybrid experiences*

4. An executable file named HybridSPSetup.exe will be downloaded to the file system.

5. Double-click HybridSPSetup.exe to install.

6. The wizard will open to connect your on-premises SharePoint Server farm with your Office 365 tenant. Click **Next** (Figure 13-6).

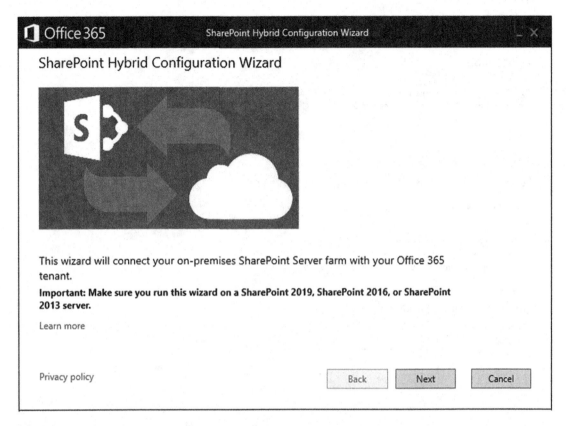

Figure 13-6. *Connecting your on-premises SharePoint Server farm with your Office 365 tenant*

7.   To set up a hybrid environment for SharePoint or OneDrive for Business (OD4B), you need to provide administrator credentials for both SharePoint server on-premises and Office 365.

8.   Click **Next** (Figure 13-7).

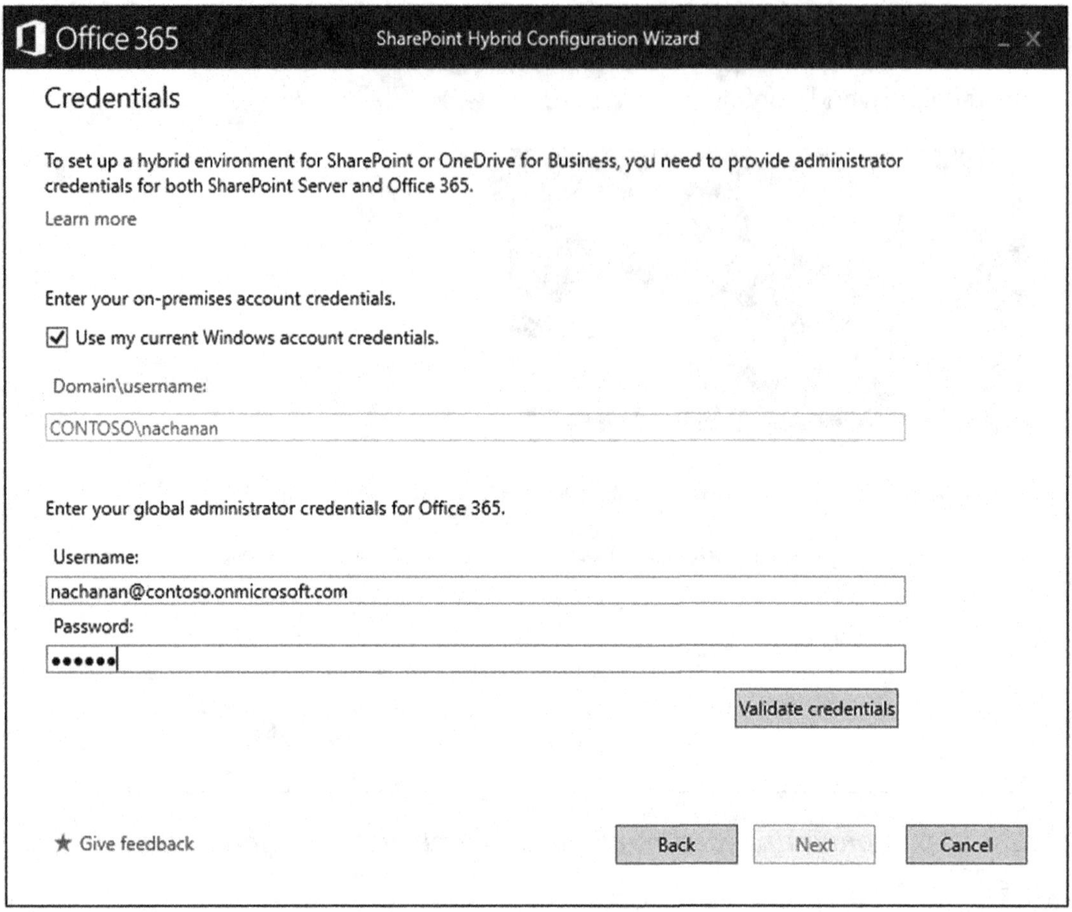

Figure 13-7. *Providing administrator credentials*

9.   A prerequisites check report will be generated (Figure 13-8).

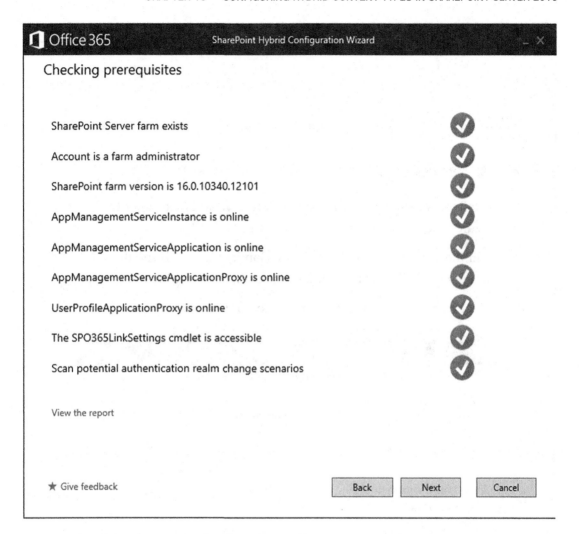

Figure 13-8. *Prerequisites check report*

In case of any errors regarding the SPO365LinkSettings cmdlet, please follow these steps and rerun the SharePoint Hybrid Configuration Wizard:

- Open the **SharePoint 2019 Management Shell** with administrator privileges.

- Run the following command (shown in Figure 13-9):

```
Set-SPO365LinkSettings -MySiteHostUrl "http://mysites.
contoso.com" -RedirectSites $true
```

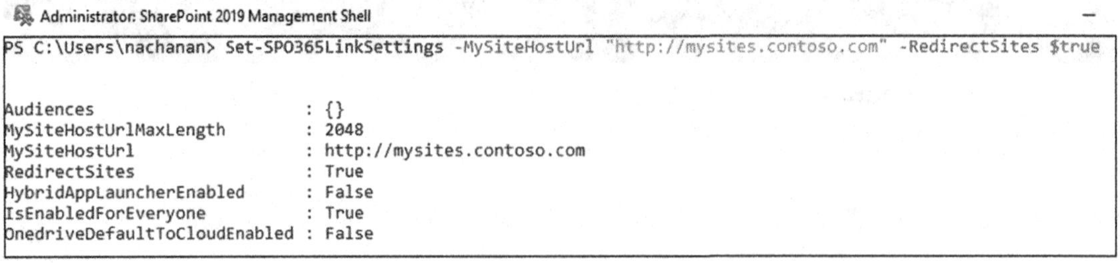

```
Administrator: SharePoint 2019 Management Shell                                          —
PS C:\Users\nachanan> Set-SPO365LinkSettings -MySiteHostUrl "http://mysites.contoso.com" -RedirectSites $true


Audiences                   : {}
MySiteHostUrlMaxLength      : 2048
MySiteHostUrl               : http://mysites.contoso.com
RedirectSites               : True
HybridAppLauncherEnabled    : False
IsEnabledForEveryone        : True
OnedriveDefaultToCloudEnabled : False
```

Figure 13-9. *Set SPO365 Link Settings*

10. Install the default features available in the Hybrid Environment
    Wizard. The configuration wizard will run.

11. After the successful run of the Hybrid Configuration Wizard, the
    SharePoint server environment will be connected to Office 365.

12. Select **Hybrid taxonomy and content type** (Figure 13-10).

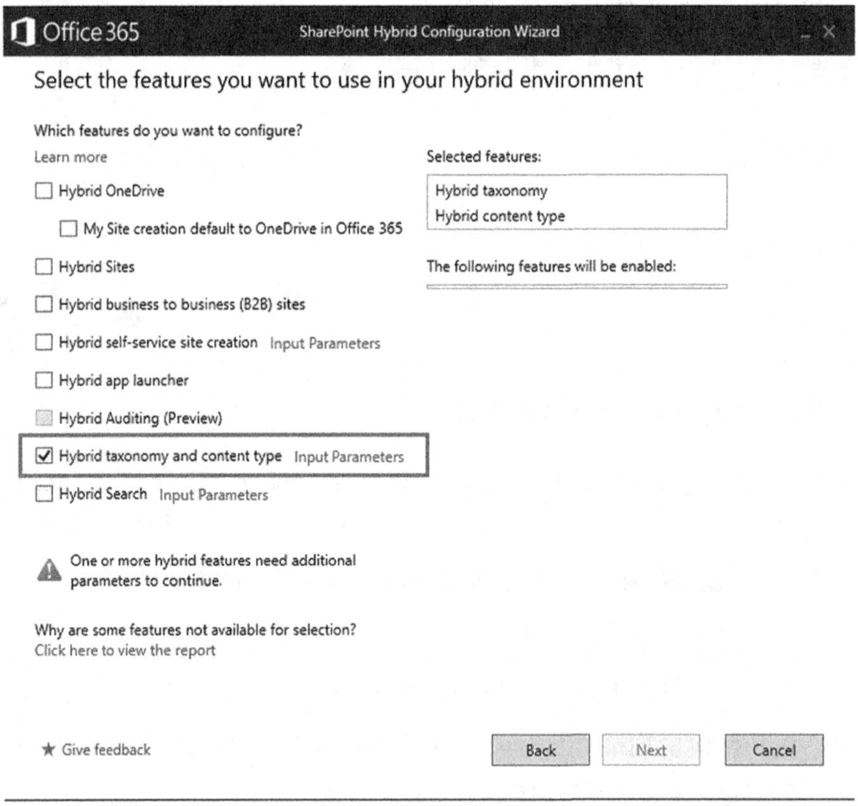

Figure 13-10. *Selecting the hybrid taxonomy and content type*

140

13.   Click **Input parameters** (Figure 13-11).

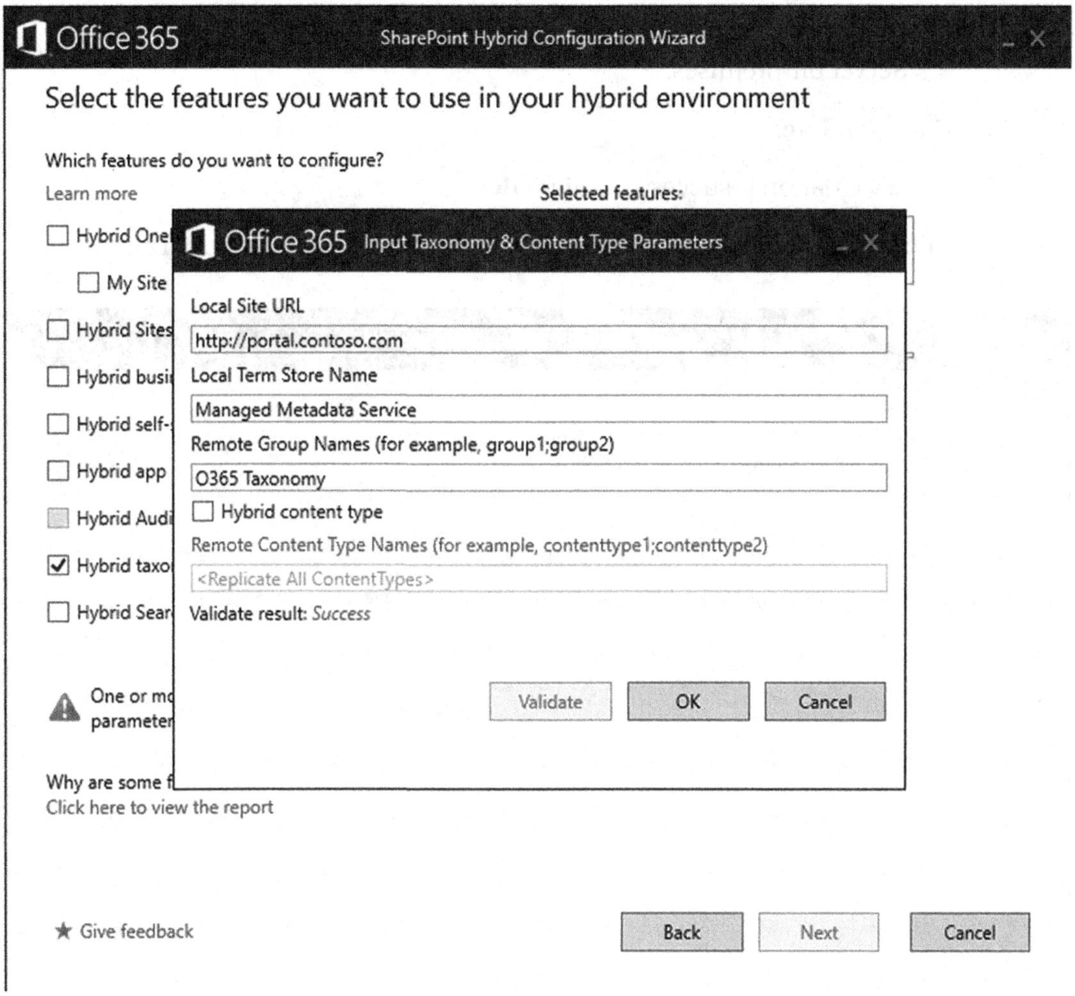

Figure 13-11. *Clicking the input parameters*

- In the **Local Site URL** field, specify the SharePoint server on-premises site URL.

- In the **Local Term Store Name** field, specify the SharePoint server on-premises managed service application name.

- Check the box for **Hybrid content type.**

- In the **Remote content type** field, specify the SharePoint online content types to be used for the hybrid. If kept blank, all the SharePoint Online content types will be replicated to SharePoint Server on-premises.

14. Click **Validate**.

15. Once validation is successful, click **OK**.

16. Click **Next**. The Hybrid Configuration Wizard will run (Figure 13-12).

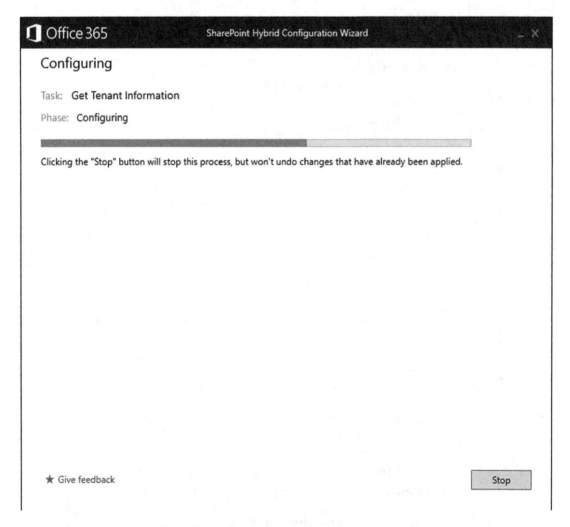

Figure 13-12. *Hybrid Configuration Wizard*

17. Upon a successful run of the SharePoint Hybrid Configuration
     Wizard, the configuration summary will be shown (Figure 13-13).

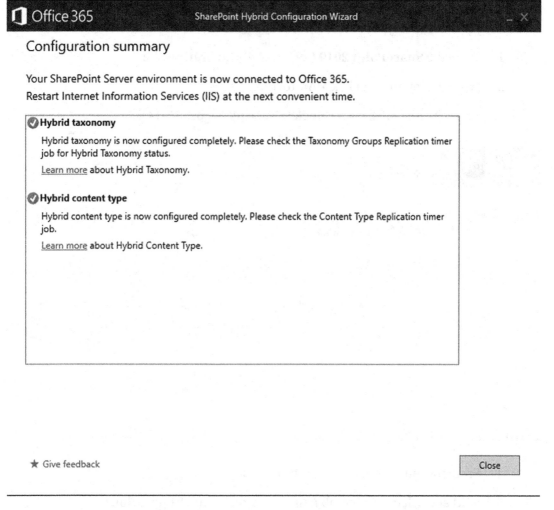

Figure 13-13. Configuration summary

18. Click **Close**.

19. Perform **IISReset** on the SharePoint Server on-premises.

Timer Job

Now, return to the SharePoint Server on-premises site and verify if the content types from SharePoint Online have been replicated. Most of them will not yet be replicated because hybrid content types run as a SharePoint timer job.

1. Open the **SharePoint 2019 Central Administration** site.

2. From the left menu, click **Monitoring**.

3. Under **Timer Jobs**, click **Check job status** (Figure 13-14).

Figure 13-14. Checking the job status

4. From the left menu, click **Job Definitions**.

5. Find and select a timer job named **Content Type Replication** (Figure 13-15).

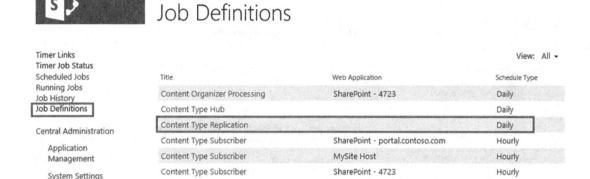

Figure 13-15. *Selecting the timer job named Content Type Replication*

6. Run the timer job by clicking **Run Now**.

7. From the left menu, click **Running Jobs**. Wait for the timer job to finish running (Figure 13-16).

Figure 13-16. *Clicking the Running Jobs button*

Verifying the Content Types Replication

1. Open the **SharePoint Server** on-premises site.

2. Navigate to **Site Settings**.

3. Under **Site Collection Administration**, click **Content type publishing**.

4. The content type hub from SharePoint Online will be listed (Figure 13-17).

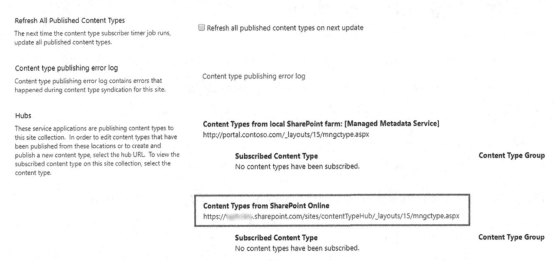

Figure 13-17. Content type hub from SharePoint Online

Conclusion

The SharePoint hybrid content types help to maintain a single set of content types across SharePoint Server on-premises and SharePoint Online. The hybrid content types replicate the content types directly to the SharePoint Server on-premises site collection rather than to the content type hub.

In the next chapter, you will explore how to configure cloud hybrid search and search content from on-premises on SharePoint Online.

CHAPTER 14

Configuring Cloud Hybrid Search

Cloud hybrid search enables users to search the content from SharePoint Server on-premises on SharePoint Online. This provides users a seamless search experience with the content being searched from on-premises and online in one place.

In this chapter, you will explore how to configure cloud hybrid search and search content from on-premises on SharePoint Online.

Cloud Hybrid Search Overview

The content is crawled from the SharePoint Server 2019 on-premises server and the index is maintained at SharePoint Online. When you have cloud hybrid search set up and a full crawl of SharePoint Server 2019 on-premises content is completed, the Microsoft 365 search center starts displaying hybrid results from the M365 index (Figure 14-1).

© Nanddeep Sadanand Nachan and Smita Sadanand Nachan 2020
N. S. Nachan and S. S. Nachan, *Understanding Hybrid Environments in SharePoint 2019*,
https://doi.org/10.1007/978-1-4842-6050-0_14

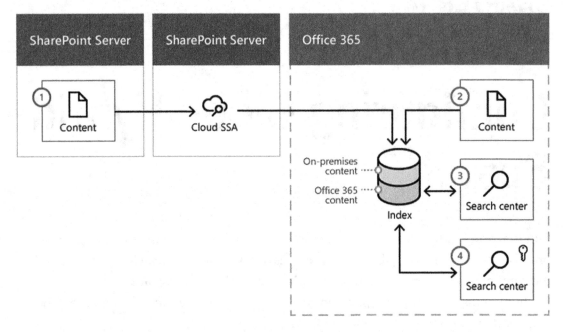

Figure 14-1. *Cloud hybrid search overview Image source: docs.microsoft.com*

Hybrid search results are shown in the following way:

1. During the crawl, metadata for on-premises content is added to the M365 search index.

2. During the crawl, metadata for Microsoft 365 content is added to the M365 search index.

3. In the search center, you create a custom result source to return search results only from M365 content.

4. The default result source shows the results from both on-premises and M365 content.

Search Experience from the End User Perspective

The following are a few important points to consider from the end user experience:

- **Search verticals:** They are important for targeting the search results against a specific set of content (e.g. videos, images, etc.). You will have to recreate your on-premises search verticals in SharePoint Online for the hybrid.

- **Site search:** When the search index is moved to Office 365, your on-premises document libraries will stop returning the results.

- **eDiscovery:** Plan to set up a separate eDiscovery in SharePoint Server on-premises and Office 365.

Planning an Architecture for Cloud Hybrid Search

The important step in setting up a cloud hybrid search is to create a cloud search service application (cloud SSA). This creates a default search architecture on the server running cloud SSA. Each SharePoint farm can have multiple SSAs but only one cloud SSA.

Search Topology

The search topology of a cloud SSA is similar to SharePoint Server on-premises SSA, except for the following few points:

- **The idle cloud SSA:** In a cloud hybrid search, M365 processes the content, generates an index, and performs analytics. This means the cloud SSA does not use its databases and components (i.e. content processing component, index component, an analytics processing component, links database, and analytics database). They are idle (Figure 14-2). The grayed-out components are inactive in a cloud hybrid search.

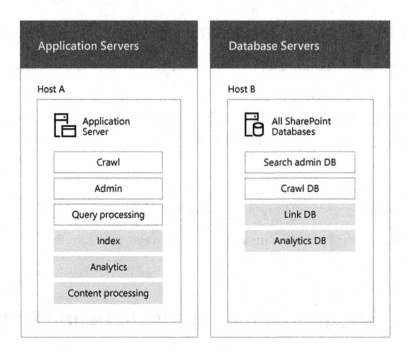

Figure 14-2. *Cloud search architecture Image source: docs.microsoft.com*

- **Search components and databases interaction:** Search
  components and databases interact differently in a cloud SSA than in
  SharePoint Server on-premises SSA (Figure 14-3).

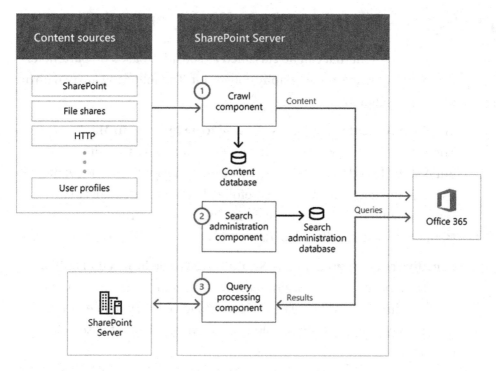

Figure 14-3. *Search components and databases interaction in cloud hybrid search*
Image source: docs.microsoft.com

The interaction between search components and databases take place as follows:

1. The crawl component gets the on-premises farm content and
    sends it to the search index in M365.

2. The search administration component runs only for the
    SharePoint Server on-premises SSA.

3. The query processing component passes on the on-premises
    search queries to the M365 index and returns the results from the
    M365 index to on-premises.

Security Trimmed Search Results

When the SharePoint Server on-premises content is crawled, the access control list
(ACL) gets crawled along with it. The ACL gets stored along with items inside the M365
search index. This helps the cloud hybrid search to recognize the same person from
on-premises against M365.

Handling On-Premises Sensitive Content

Organizations have content that can be classified as sensitive based on parameters of legal, regulatory, compliance, or geography constraint. The following are two obvious scenarios of sensitive content:

- **Sensitive content metadata is allowed to be indexed in M365:**
  There are scenarios when certain content is marked as sensitive but is still allowed in the M365 search index only for a specific set of users. In this case, you need to carefully plan the access rights to the sensitive content so that sensitive content will be returned in search results for those specific set of users.

- **Sensitive content metadata is NOT allowed to be indexed in M365:**
  This is a typical scenario where sensitive on-premises content should not be index in the M365 search index. In such cases, you need to plan for a cloud hybrid search along with a hybrid federated search (Figure 14-4).

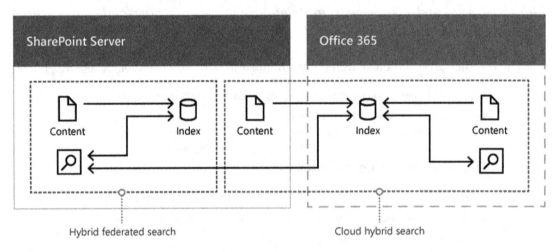

Figure 14-4. *Cloud hybrid search along with hybrid federated search Image source: docs.microsoft.com*

Plan separate content sources for sensitive data on-premises. The metadata crawled from sensitive on-premises content will be indexed to SharePoint Server.

Plan content sources for the cloud search service application (cloud SSA) to cover all SharePoint Server content except sensitive content. The crawled metadata will be added to the M365 search index.

Plan a hybrid federated search when a user needs results from the search index in M365.

Enabling a Hybrid Search Experience

Follow these steps to enable the hybrid search experience:

1. Open the **SharePoint 2019 Central Administration** site.

2. From the left navigation, click **Configuration Wizards**.

3. Under **Farm Configuration**, click **Launch the Hybrid Configuration Wizard** (Figure 14-5).

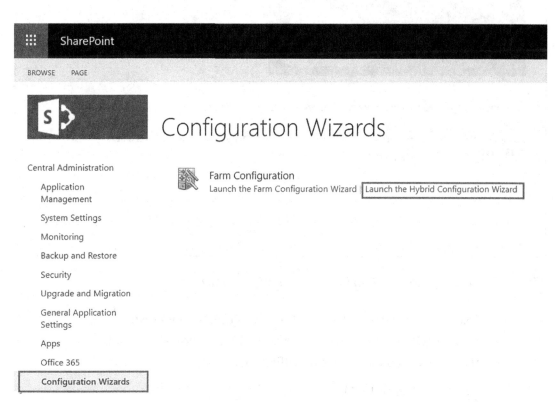

Figure 14-5. *Launching the Hybrid Configuration Wizard*

4. An executable file named HybridSPSetup.exe will be downloaded to the file system.

5. Double-click HybridSPSetup.exe to install.

6. The wizard will open to connect your on-premises SharePoint Server farm with your Office 365 tenant.

7. Click **Next** (Figure 14-6).

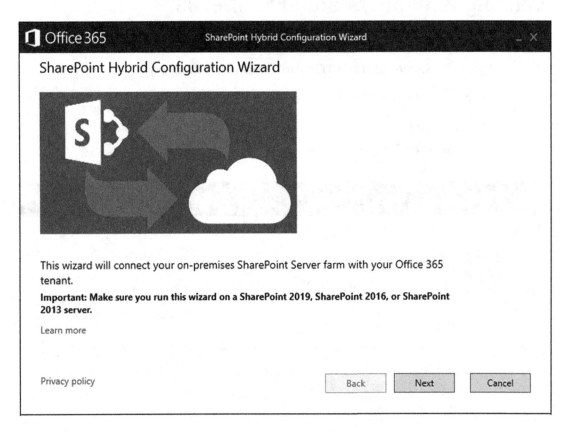

Figure 14-6. *SharePoint Hybrid Configuration Wizard*

8. To set up a hybrid environment for SharePoint or OneDrive for Business (OD4B), you need to provide administrator credentials for both SharePoint Server and Office 365.

9. Click **Next** (Figure 14-7).

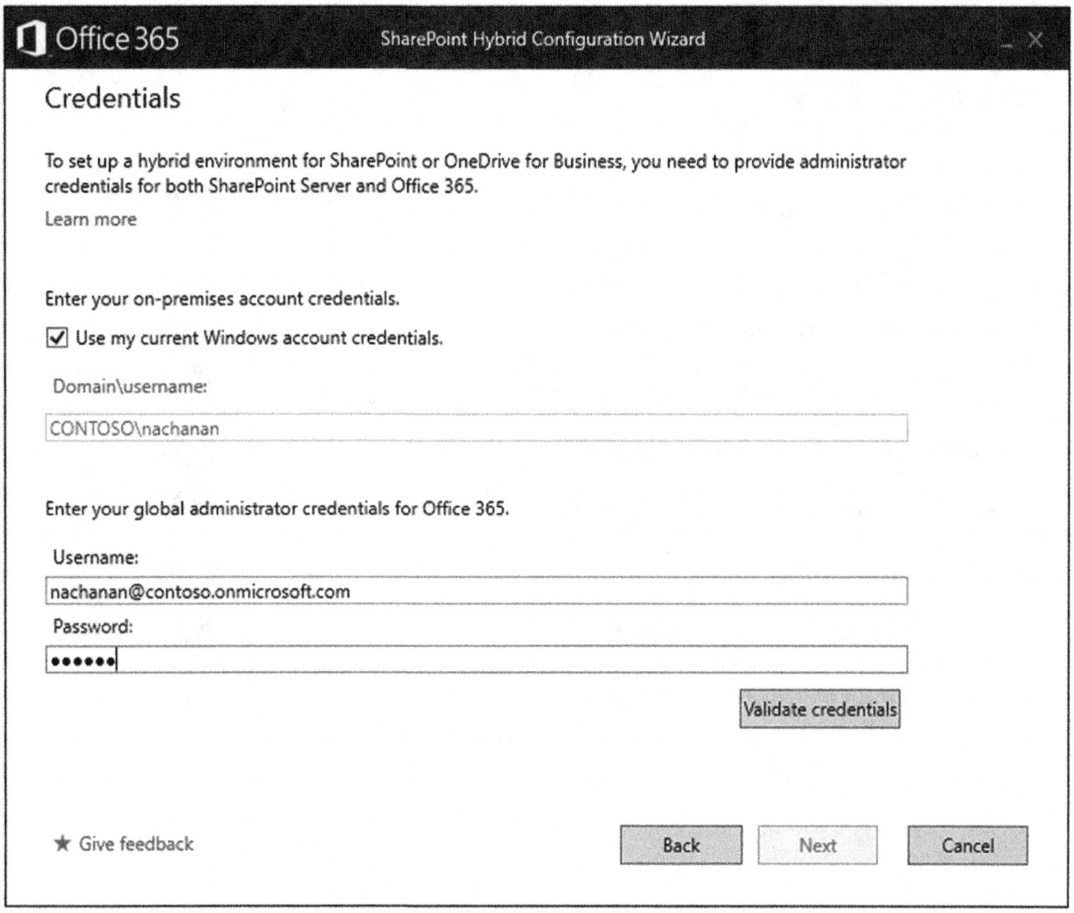

Figure 14-7. *Credentials for a hybrid environment*

10.   A prerequisites check report will be generated (Figure 14-8).

Figure 14-8. *Prerequisites check*

In case of any errors regarding the SPO365LinkSettings cmdlet, please follow these steps and rerun the SharePoint Hybrid Configuration Wizard:

- Open the SharePoint 2019 Management Shell with administrator privileges.

- Run the following command (also shown in Figure 14-9):

```
Set-SPO365LinkSettings -MySiteHostUrl "http://mysites.
contoso.com" -RedirectSites $true
```

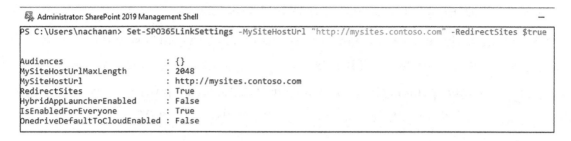

Figure 14-9. *Set SPO365 Link Settings*

11. In the **Select the features to use** screen, select **Hybrid Search**
     (Figure 14-10).

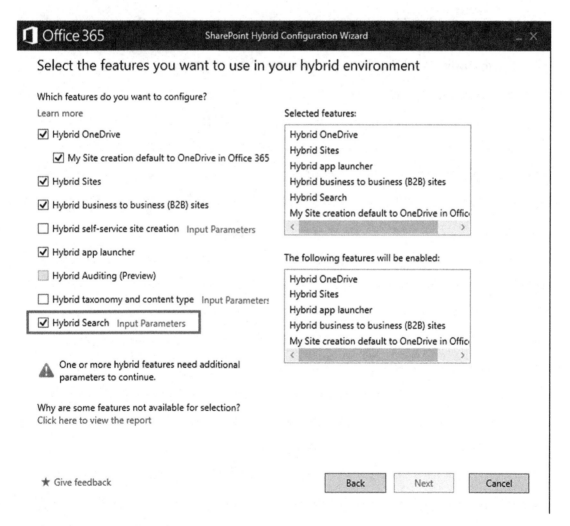

Figure 14-10. *Selecting the hybrid search feature*

12. Click **Input Parameters** next to Hybrid Search.

13. Enter the name of the on-premises SharePoint Server to host the cloud search service application.

14. If you are planning for high availability (HA) search topology, enter the name of the second on-premises SharePoint server. Leave the field empty otherwise.

15. Enter the name of the on-premises SQL database server to host the search data.

16. Enter the name of the cloud search service application to create.

17. Download and install MS Online PowerShell for Azure Active Directory and Microsoft Online Services Sign-In Assistant by following the links.

18. Click **OK** (Figure 14-11).

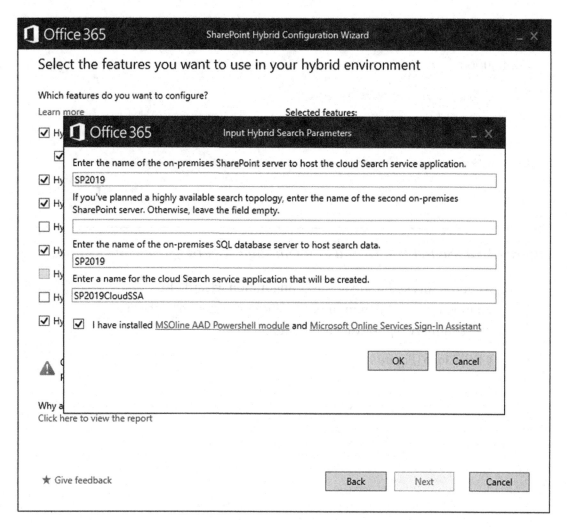

Figure 14-11. Configuring the hybrid search parameters

19. Click **Next**.

20. The configuration wizard will run (Figure 14-12).

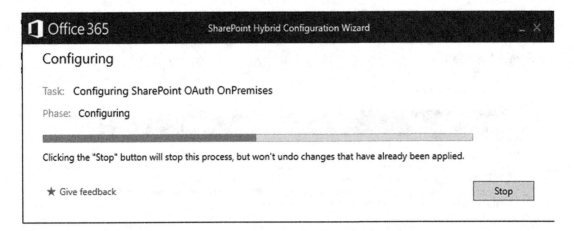

Figure 14-12. *SharePoint Hybrid Configuration Wizard*

21. After the successful run of the configuration wizard, the
     SharePoint server environment will be connected to Office 365.
     The summary report will be generated.

22. Click **Close** (Figure 14-13).

Figure 14-13. *SharePoint hybrid configuration summary*

23.   Perform **IISReset** on SharePoint Server 2019.

PowerShell Script Approach

Download Windows PowerShell scripts to configure cloud hybrid search for SharePoint from Microsoft Download Center (www.microsoft.com/en-us/download/details. aspx?id=51490).

The download contains two PowerShell scripts:

1.   CreateCloudSSA.ps1 (creates the cloud search service application)

2.   Onboard-CloudHybridSearch.ps1

Create Cloud Search Service Application: The cloud search service application crawls on-premises content for cloud hybrid search.

1. Open the **SharePoint 2019 Management Shell** with administrator privileges.

2. Navigate to the `scripts` folder.

3. Execute `CreateCloudSSA.ps1` (Figure 14-14).

```
Administrator: SharePoint 2019 Management Shell
PS C:\SP2019\Cloud_Hybrid_Search_Scripts> .\CreateCloudSSA.ps1

cmdlet CreateCloudSSA.ps1 at command pipeline position 1
Supply values for the following parameters:
SearchServerName: SP2019
SearchServiceAccount: contoso\sp_searchservice
SearchServiceAppName: Search Service Application Cloud
DatabaseServerName: SP2019
```

Figure 14-14. *Creating a cloud search service application*

Parameters used in the script:

- `SearchServerName`: SharePoint on-premises search installation server name

- `SearchServiceAccount`: SharePoint on-premises search installation admin account

- `SearchServiceAppName`: Name of the cloud search service application to be created

- `DatabaseServerName`: SharePoint on-premises database installation server name

The search service account needs to already exist in Windows Active Directory. The script will add it as a managed account, if it hasn't been added already. Please note that only one cloud SSA is supported per SharePoint farm.

Connect On-Premises Cloud Search Service Application to Office 365 tenant: You can onboard a SharePoint Online (SPO) tenant and SharePoint server cloud SSA to the cloud hybrid search by using PowerShell script named `Onboard-CloudHybridSearch.ps1`.

1. Open the **SharePoint 2019 Management Shell** with administrator privileges.

2. Navigate to the `scripts` folder.

3. Execute `Onboard-CloudHybridSearch.ps1` (Figure 14-15).

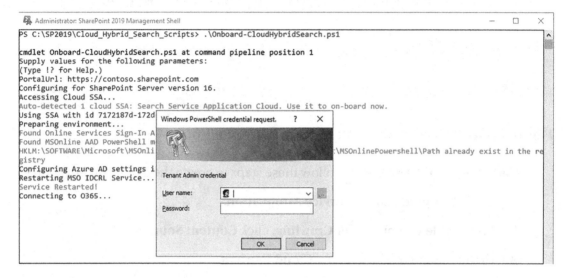

Figure 14-15. *Connecting the on-premises cloud SSA to an Office 365 tenant*

Parameters used in the script:

- `PortalUrl`: SharePoint Online portal URL, such as `https://contoso.sharepoint.com`

- `CloudSsaId`: Name or id (GUID) of the cloud search service application, created with the CreateCloudSSA script. The `CreateCloudSSA.ps1` script will output this information after its successful execution.

- `Credential`: Logon credential for the Office 365 tenant admin (will prompt for credential if not specified)

On-Premises Cloud Search Service Application Configuration

Verifying the On-Premises Cloud Search Service Application: Follow these steps to verify the on-premises cloud search service application:

1. Open the **SharePoint 2019 Central Administration** site.

2. Under **Application Management**, click **Manage service applications**.

3. Verify that the Cloud Search Service Application exists (Figure 14-16).

Name	Type	Status
Search Administration Web Service for Search Service Application Cloud	Search Administration Web Service Application	Started
Search Administration Web Service for Search Service Application	Search Administration Web Service Application	Started
Search Service Application Cloud	Search Service Application	Started
Search Service Application Cloud_proxy	Search Service Application Proxy	Started
Search Service Application	Search Service Application	Started
Search Service Application	Search Service Application Proxy	Started

Figure 14-16. *On-premises cloud search service application*

Create Cloud Content Source: Follow these steps to create the cloud content source:

1. Click the **Cloud Search Service Application**.

2. From the left menu, under **Crawling**, click **Content Sources**.

3. Create a new content source - **Cloud Content**.

4. Add the SharePoint 2019 on-premises site under site addresses to crawl.

5. Define an incremental and full crawl schedule.

6. Click **OK**.

7. Run the full crawl manually for the first time (Figure 14-17).

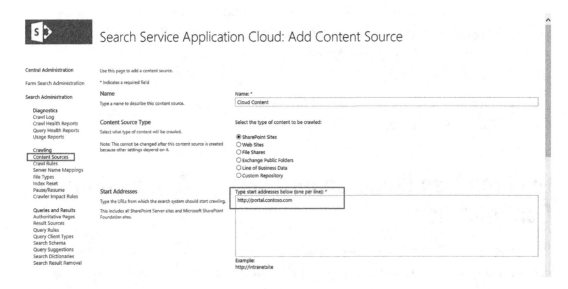

Figure 14-17. *Creating a cloud content source*

Verifying a Hybrid Search

Follow these steps to verify a hybrid search configuration:

1. Open the **SharePoint Online** site.

2. Search **IsExternalContent: 1** to see the external content (i.e. content from SharePoint 2019 on-premises, as shown in Figure 14-18).

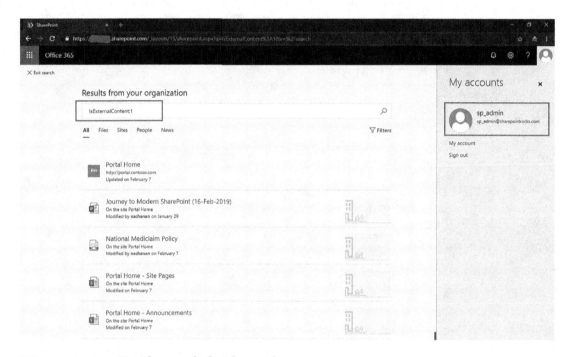

Figure 14-18. *Verifying a hybrid search*

Conclusion

The hybrid search can be enabled between SharePoint on-premises and SharePoint Online. The cloud search service application crawls on-premises content for a cloud hybrid search.

In the next chapter, you will explore the concept behind on-premises data gateways, when to use them, installation, and configuration.

CHAPTER 15

On-Premises Data Gateway

An on-premises data gateway is a bridge for quick and secure data transfer between an on-premises environment and cloud services. These cloud services include Power BI, Power Apps, and Power Automate from the O365 stack as well as Azure Analysis Services and Azure Logic Apps. In recent times, there have been increasing installs of on-premises data gateways to achieve hybrid scenarios. In this chapter, you will explore the concept behind on-premises data gateways, when to use them, installation, and configuration.

On-Premises Data Gateway

Hybrid environments are very common across organizations because they bring the best of both on-premises and cloud features. An on-premises data gateway is one gateway for multiple cloud services and experiences including the following (see also Figure 15-1):

- Power BI
- Power BI dataflows
- Power Apps
- Power Automate
- Azure Analysis Services
- Logic Apps
- Microsoft Search

© Nanddeep Sadanand Nachan and Smita Sadanand Nachan 2020
N. S. Nachan and S. S. Nachan, *Understanding Hybrid Environments in SharePoint 2019*,
https://doi.org/10.1007/978-1-4842-6050-0_15

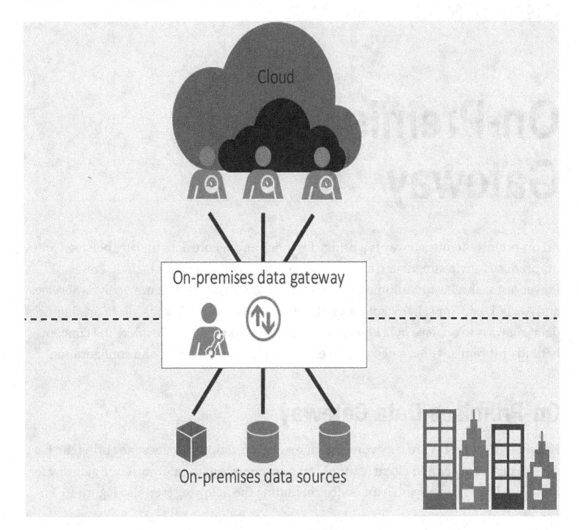

Figure 15-1. *On-premises data gateway Image source: docs.microsoft.com*

By using an on-premises data gateway, organizations can keep data sources and databases in their on-premises environments and can also securely use that on-premises data in cloud services.

Do You Always Need a Data Gateway?

No. You don't need a data gateway in all scenarios. If the data source is located in the on-premises network, you will need a gateway. For online or cloud-based data sources, a data gateway is not needed (Figure 15-2).

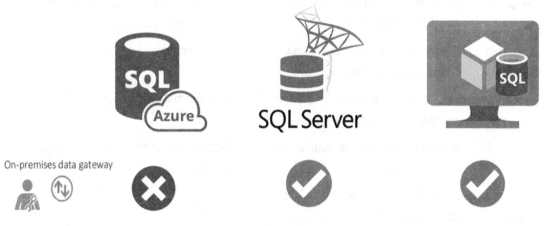

Figure 15-2. *On-premises scenarios*

For example,

- If you are getting data from an Azure SQL DB, you don't need a gateway.

- If you are getting data from a SQL Server database located on your local domain server, you need a gateway.

- However, a SQL Server database located on an Azure Virtual Machine is considered on-premises and needs a gateway.

Modes of On-Premises Data Gateways

The data gateway offers two modes: standard mode and personal mode. It is worth a mention that both are free to use and do not involve any licensing cost. Table 15-1 differentiates the modes and how you want to use them.

Table 15-1. *Data Gateway Modes and Uses*

	Standard mode	**Personal mode**
Target users	Enterprises with central data source management and access control	Business analysts
Use case	Admin sets up data gateway for employees in an organization	Set up and use the data gateway for personal data sources only
Supported features	Direct query (for all services) and scheduled refresh (only for Power BI)	Import with scheduled refresh
	Each data source should be explicitly configured by a gateway admin	No additional data source configuration is needed
	Centralized data source management and access control	Data source connections are managed per user
Supported services	Power BI, Power Apps, Power Automate, Azure Logic Apps, Azure Analysis Services, Power Query Online with CDS	Power BI

Standard Mode: The standard mode allows multiple users to connect to multiple on-premises data sources. It is the recommended mode of installation. Multiple developers can use a gateway installed in standard mode. A dedicated gateway admin manages the data gateway for the team and can authorize multiple developers to use the same gateway. The standard mode offers more centralized control and monitoring options.

Personal Mode: The personal mode allows a single user to connect to the data sources, which cannot be shared. This mode can be used to connect to local data sources like SQL Server or Excel. This gateway mode only supports Power BI for importing data or scheduling refresh connections. Since only one developer can use this gateway, it is called a personal mode. This gateway is more suitable for business analysts who create reports, connect to this gateway, and share the reports with multiple users.

Data Gateway Installation

The installation of the gateway enables on-premises-to-cloud data connections. It can be installed centrally and used to manage data connections for cloud services. You can register a new gateway or migrate/restore an existing gateway.

Follow these steps to install the gateway:

1. Download and install the standard gateway from this URL:

   `https://go.microsoft.com/fwlink/?LinkId=2116849&clcid=`
   `0x409`

2. Review the minimum requirements before you proceed with the gateway installation (Figure 15-3).

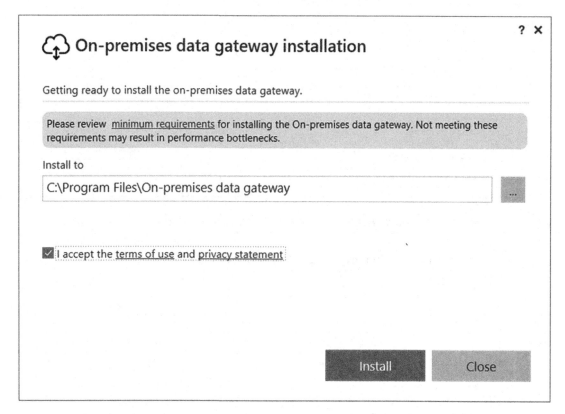

Figure 15-3. *On-premises data gateway requirements*

3. Optionally, change the default installation location.

4. Select **I accept the terms of use and privacy statement**.

5. Click **Install**.

6. The installation wizard will run (Figure 15-4).

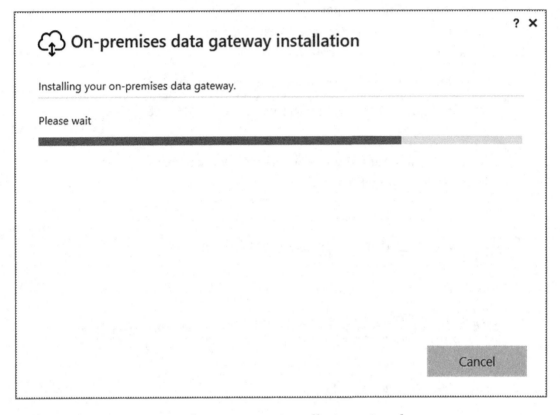

Figure 15-4. *On-premises data gateway installation wizard*

7. Provide an Office 365 organization account email address (Figure 15-5).

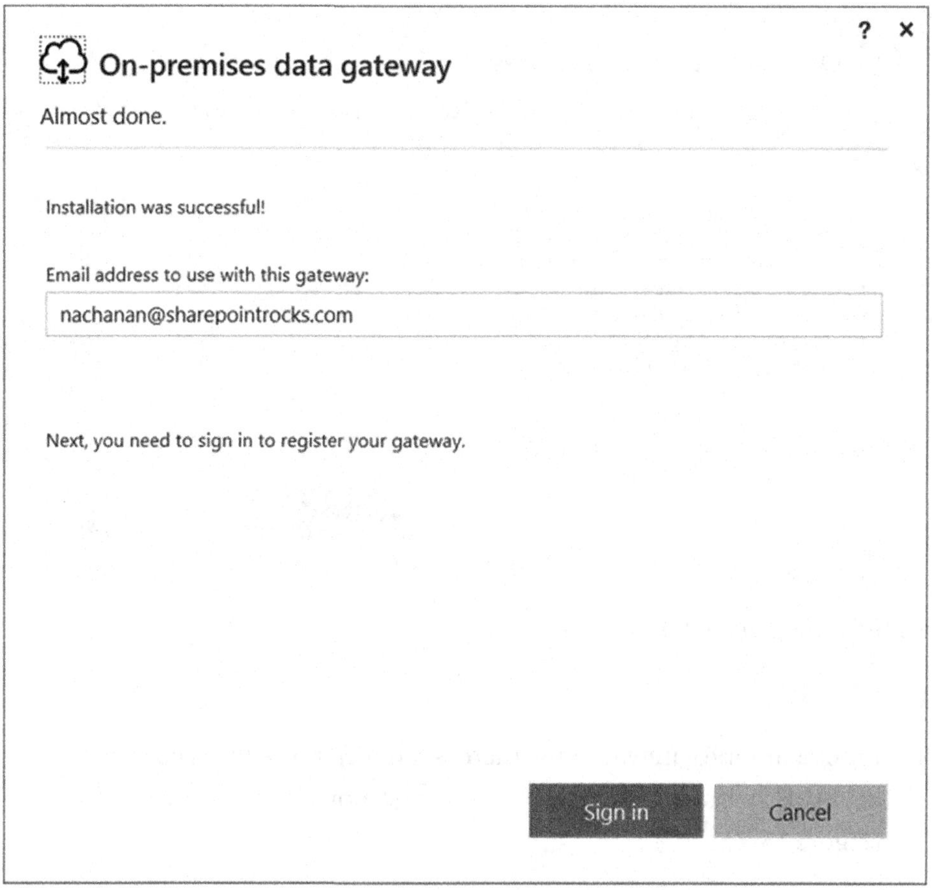

Figure 15-5. Signing in with an Office 365 organization account email address

8. Click **Sign in**.

9. Select **Register a new gateway on this computer** (Figure 15-6).

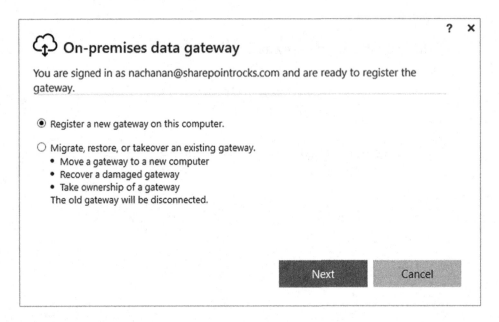

Figure 15-6. *Registering a new gateway*

10. Click **Next**.

11. Enter a unique gateway name (across tenant). Enter the recovery
     key. This key is useful when recovering or moving the gateway
     (Figure 15-7).

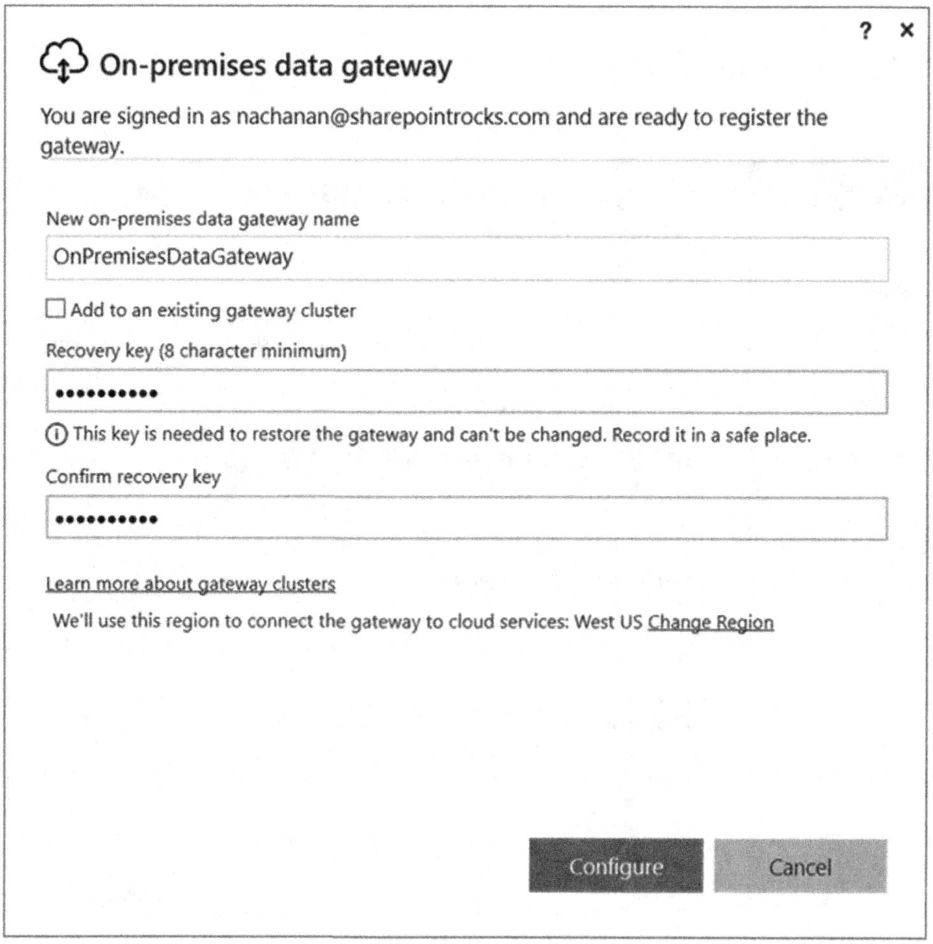

Figure 15-7. Registering a new gateway

12. The **Add to an existing gateway cluster** checkbox is helpful to configure a gateway cluster.

13. Click **Configure**.

14. The gateway is now online and ready to use (Figure 15-8).

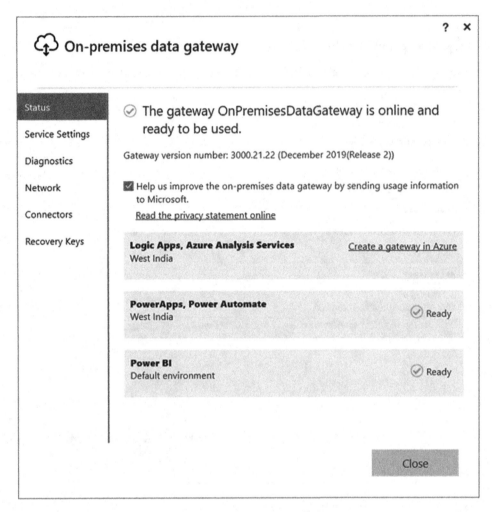

Figure 15-8. *The gateway is online and ready to use*

Gateway App Features

Once the data gateway is up and running, it provides various features that can be accessed from the left-hand menu of the gateway app. Table 15-2 shows the important available features.

Table 15-2. *Data Gateway Features*

Tab	Service	Description
Status	Gateway cluster status	Displays the status of the gateway cluster (e.g. online), gateway version, and a list of cloud services associated with the gateway
Service Settings	Restart the gateway	Restarts the gateway after any configuration changes
Service Settings	Gateway service account	Defines Windows service sign-in credentials. The default account is NT SERVICE\PBIEgwService.
Diagnostics	Additional logging	Turn on this feature to get additional verbose information in the log file about the usage of a gateway.
Diagnostics	Gateway logs	Provides a consolidated gateway log in a .zip format
Diagnostics	Network ports test	Confirms whether a gateway can access the required ports for its functioning
Network	Network status	Defines whether a gateway can reach outside of your network
Network	HTTPS mode	Defines communication mode with Azure Service Bus as HTTPS or TCP
Connectors	Custom data connectors	Defines custom connectors for Power BI reports
Recovery Keys	Recovery keys	Allows changing the recovery key defined during installation

Gateway Considerations

The following are a few important points to note for gateway installations:

1. Install a gateway on any domain-joined machine. However, do not install it on a domain controller.

2. The gateway should always be up and running to process the requests. So, never turn off the machine running the gateway.

3. The machine hosting the gateway should always be connected to the internet.

4. Gateway performance may diminish over a wireless network.

5. A gateway, once installed, automatically provisions Azure Service
    bus relays.

Data Gateway Architecture

The data gateway, once installed on a computer, runs as a Windows service named
on-premises data gateway. This service is registered with a cloud service via the Azure
service bus (Figure 15-9).

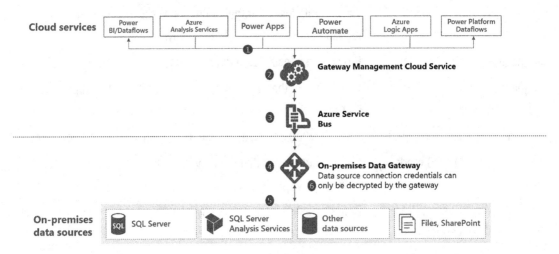

Figure 15-9. *Data gateway architecture Image source: docs.microsoft.com*

The queries and data flow take place as follows:

1. A cloud service queries for the on-premises data source using
    encrypted credentials.

2. The query is analyzed by the gateway cloud service and is passed
    on to the Azure service bus.

3. The on-premises data gateway continuously polls the Azure
    service bus.

4. Once the on-premises data gateway gets the query, it connects to
    the on-premises data sources by decrypting the credentials.

5. The query is executed by the on-premises data source.

6. The results are sent back to the gateway and in turn to the cloud service.

Configuring High Availability for Gateway Clusters

To avoid a single point of failure and to load balance the traffic, you can define an on-premises data gateway cluster (Figure 15-10).

Figure 15-10. Configuring a gateway cluster

The **Add to an existing gateway cluster** checkbox is helpful to configure a gateway cluster.

High Availability: High availability (HA) can be achieved by adding new members to the gateway cluster. During the gateway installation, you can join an existing gateway cluster using the recovery key. Only the administrator of the original gateway can add new members to an existing gateway cluster (Figure 15-11).

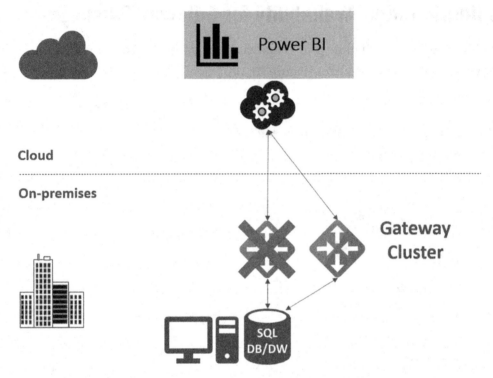

Figure 15-11. *High availability in a gateway cluster Image source: docs.microsoft. com*

With high availability in place, if one data gateway goes down, another one can handle the requests, as shown in Figure 15-11.

Load Balancing: A gateway cluster automatically balances the traffic across all available gateways in a cluster. Please note that offline gateway members negatively impact the performance.

Gateway Administration

Power Platform Admin Portal: Office 365 provides a unified portal for administering power portals and data gateways at https://admin.powerplatform.microsoft.com.

Gateway Management PowerShell: The on-premises data gateway cmdlets for Windows PowerShell (`https://aka.ms/GatewayPowerShell`) help administer the gateways.

A few commonly used cmdlets are as follows:

- Return all gateways within your tenant:

  ```
  Get-DataGatewayCluster -Scope Organization
  ```

- Return a list of gateways for which you are the administrator:

  ```
  Get-DataGatewayCluster -Scope Individual
  ```

- Restrict installation of an on-premises data gateway:

  ```
  Set-DataGatewayTenantPolicy
  -ResourceGatewayInstallPolicy Restricted
  ```

Conclusion

An on-premises data gateway is a bridge for quick and secure data transfer between the on-premises environment and cloud services including Power BI, Power Apps, Power Automate, Azure Analysis Services, and Azure Logic Apps. By using an on-premises data gateway, organizations can keep data sources and databases in their on-premises environments and will still be able to securely use that on-premises data in the cloud services.

In the next chapter, you will explore how to integrate Power BI reporting with SharePoint Server 2019 on-premises using the data gateway.

CHAPTER 16

Power BI Integration with SharePoint Server 2019

SharePoint Server 2019 supports integration with Power BI, which is one of the rich cloud features made available on-premises. The introduction of Power BI to SharePoint Server 2019 on-premises is one of the major enhancements in BI.

In this chapter, you will explore how to integrate Power BI reporting with SharePoint Server 2019 on-premises using a data gateway.

Power BI Overview

Power BI helps to turn unrelated sources of data into interactive insights. Power BI allows you to connect to various data sources and create interactive reports. Power BI consists of a Windows desktop application called Power BI Desktop and an online SAAS service called Power BI Service.

Power BI Data Refresh Architecture

The data gateway helps to connect the SharePoint Server 2019 on-premises data sources with Power BI to create interactive reports. Figure 16-1 shows the underlying architecture of Power BI on-premises data refresh.

© Nanddeep Sadanand Nachan and Smita Sadanand Nachan 2020
N. S. Nachan and S. S. Nachan, *Understanding Hybrid Environments in SharePoint 2019*,
https://doi.org/10.1007/978-1-4842-6050-0_16

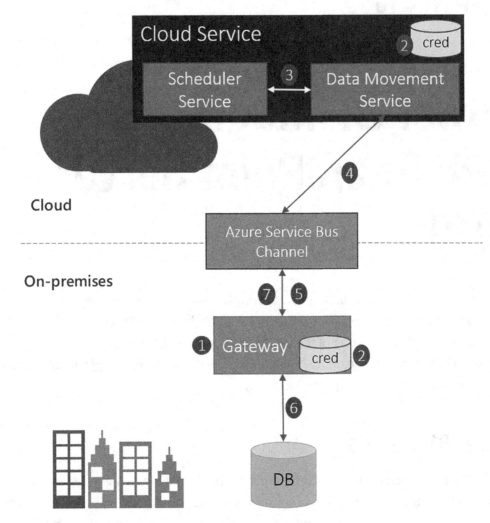

Figure 16-1. *Power BI data refresh architecture*

The Power BI on-premises data refresh takes place in the following way:

1. When a data gateway is installed and configured, a dedicated
    Azure Service Bus channel is automatically configured.

2. Credentials entered for the data source in the cloud services are
    encrypted, tested, and then stored encrypted. Only the associated
    gateway (cluster) can decrypt the credentials. The Power BI
    Personal Gateway keeps credentials on-premises only.

3. One of the supported cloud services kicks off a refresh or a live query.

4. The Data Movement Service analyzes the query and pushes it to the appropriate Service Bus communication channel.

5. The gateway polls its Service Bus channel for pending requests. It takes the pending request.

6. The gateway fetches the query, decrypts the credentials, and sends a query to the data source for execution.

7. Upon query execution, the gateway securely streams the data compressed to the cloud service.

Installing an On-Premises Data Gateway (Personal Mode)

In the previous chapter, you explored how to install an on-premises data gateway in standard mode. Now, you will explore the option of installing a data gateway in a personal mode, which is only mode supported in Power BI.

On-premises gateways allow connecting to on-premises data sources without the need to move the data. This provides the flexibility to query large datasets. The on-premises data gateway (personal mode) allows individuals to install a gateway on their computer and gain access to on-premises data.

Follow these steps to install an on-premises data gateway in personal mode:

1. Log into the **Power BI** site (`https://powerbi.microsoft.com`). The sign-in account could be an Office 365 account (either a work account or a school account).

2. Click **Download ➤ Data Gateway** (Figure 16-2).

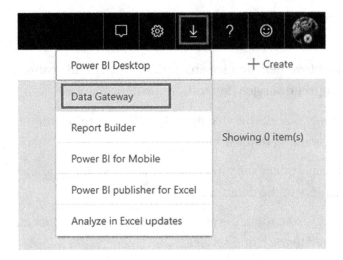

Figure 16-2. *Power BI data gateway*

3.   Click **Download personal mode** ➤ (Figure 16-3).

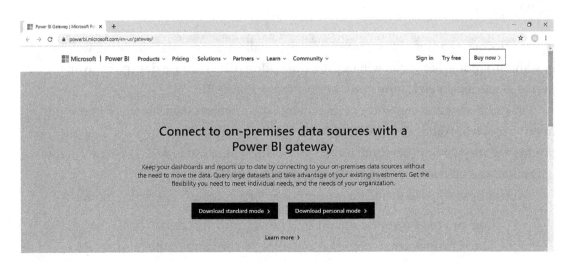

Figure 16-3. *Downloading a data gateway*

4.   The on-premises data gateway (personal mode).exe file will be downloaded to your system. Double-click the file to start the installation wizard.

5.   If required, change the default installation location.

6. Select **I accept the terms of use and privacy statement**.

7. Click **Install** (Figure 16-4).

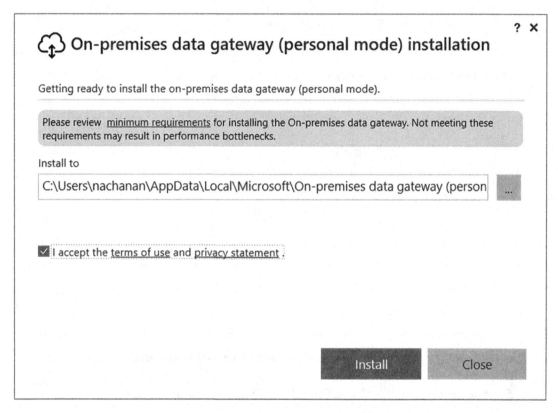

Figure 16-4. *Data gateway (personal mode) installation*

8. The installation wizard will run (Figure 16-5).

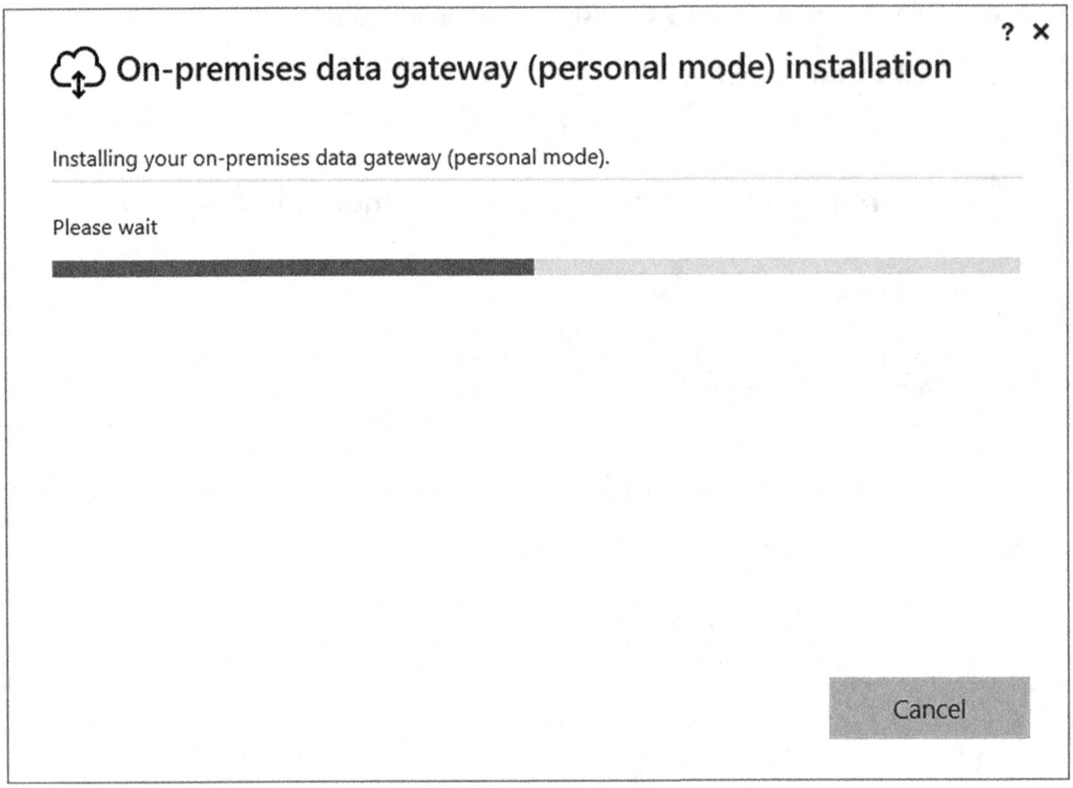

Figure 16-5. *Data gateway (personal mode) installation wizard*

9. Specify the email address. Provide an Office 365 organization account email address.

10. Click **Sign in** (Figure 16-6).

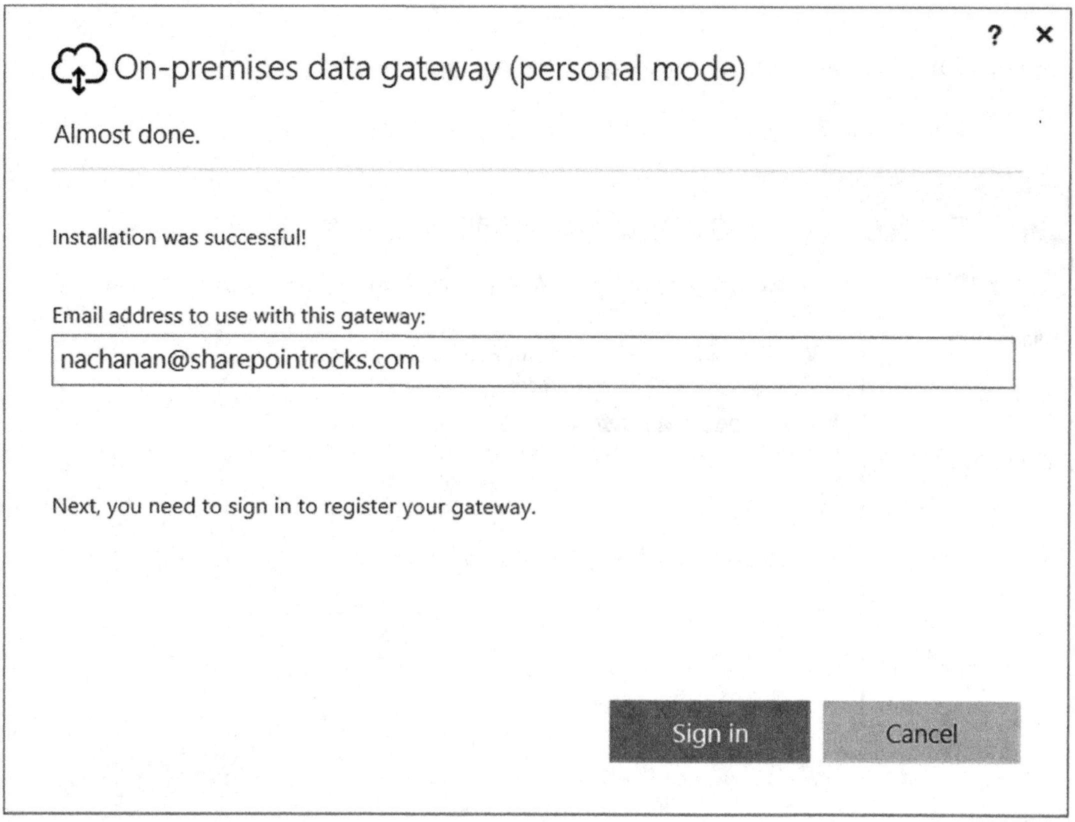

Figure 16-6. *Sign in with an Office 365 organization account email address*

11. Once installed, the on-premises gateway is ready to use in personal mode (Figure 16-7).

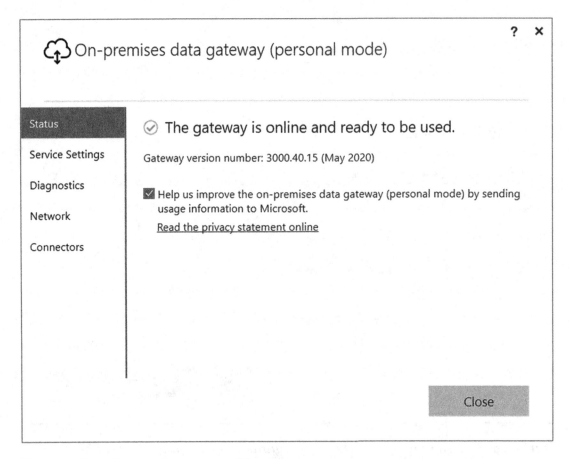

Figure 16-7. *Data gateway install location*

Connecting to an On-Premises Data Source

You can connect to the above created on-premises data source from the Power BI desktop to create meaningful reports. Follow these steps to connect to the on-premises data source:

1. Download and install Power BI Desktop from `https://powerbi.microsoft.com/en-us/desktop/`.

2. From the Home Menu, click **Get Data ➤ More...** (Figure 16-8).

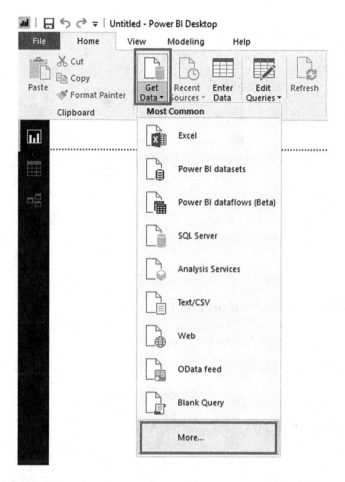

Figure 16-8. *Getting data from more sources*

3. In the **Get Data** screen, type **SharePoint**.

4. Select the **SharePoint list** option.

5. Click **Connect** (Figure 16-9).

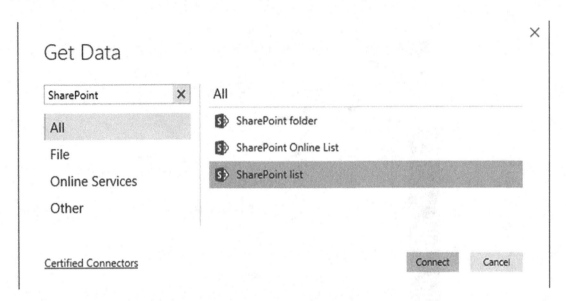

Figure 16-9. *Getting SharePoint on-premises data*

6. Enter the SharePoint Server 2019 site URL.

7. Click **OK** (Figure 16-10).

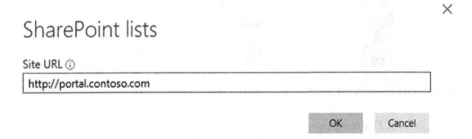

Figure 16-10. *SharePoint Server 2019 site URL*

8. Select the list and click **Load** (Figure 16-11).

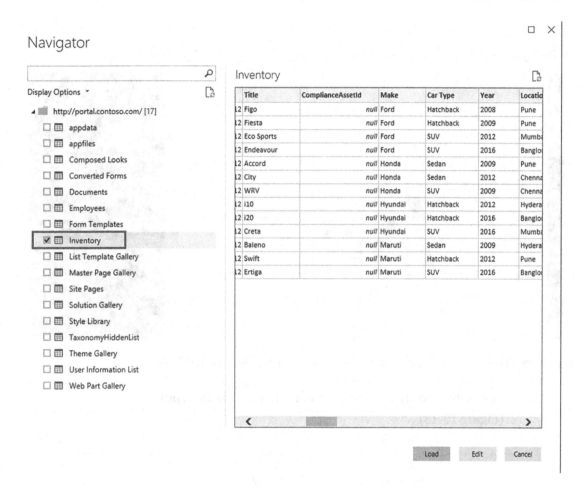

Figure 16-11. *Loading a list from the SharePoint Server 2019 site*

9. Create a report and publish it (Figure 16-12).

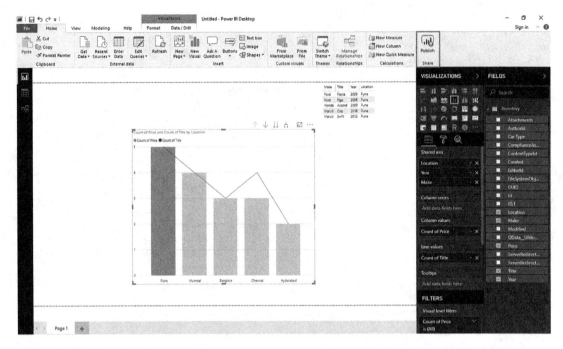

Figure 16-12.   *Power BI report from SharePoint Server 2019 data*

10. Select the already created workspace to publish the report
(Figure 16-13).

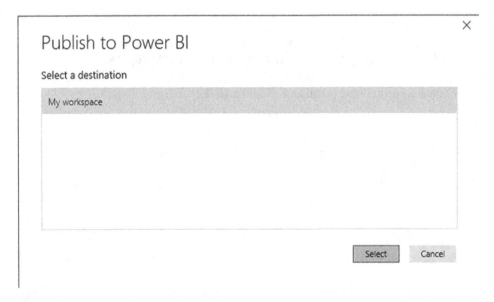

Figure 16-13.   *Selecting a destination workspace to publish the Power BI report*

11.   Under **My Workspaces**, click **Datasets**.

12.   Select the dataset you created (e.g. Inventory).

13.   You now have an on-premises data gateway as well as a personal
      mode gateway (Figure 16-14).

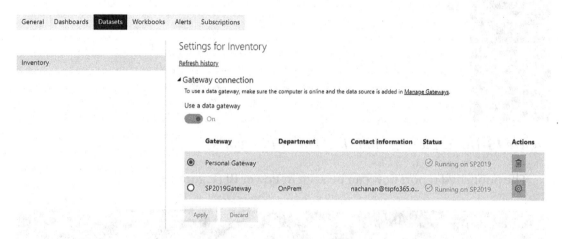

Figure 16-14. *Choosing a dataset*

Exploring Power BI Reports

Follow these steps to explore the published Power BI reports:

1.   Under **My Workspace**, click **Reports**.

2.   Click the report name you created (e.g. Inventory), as shown in
     Figure 16-15.

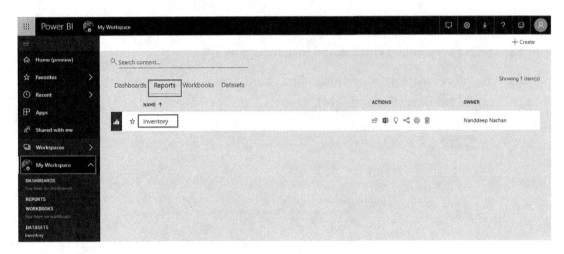

Figure 16-15. *Exploring published Power BI reports*

The published report now can be seen in Power BI (Figure 16-16).

Figure 16-16. *Published Power BI report*

Publishing the Power BI Report to the Web (Power BI Service)

The Power BI Report does not have the **Embed in SharePoint** option offered in SharePoint Online. However, you can use the **Publish to web** option. Open the report in the Power BI web site (`powerbi.microsoft.com`), if not already, and then publish it to the Web.

Follow these steps to publish the Power BI report:

1. Click **File ➤ Publish to web** (Figure 16-17).

Figure 16-17. *Publishing the Power BI report to the Web*

2. The generated embed code can be used on a SharePoint Server 2019 on-premises site (Figure 16-18).

197

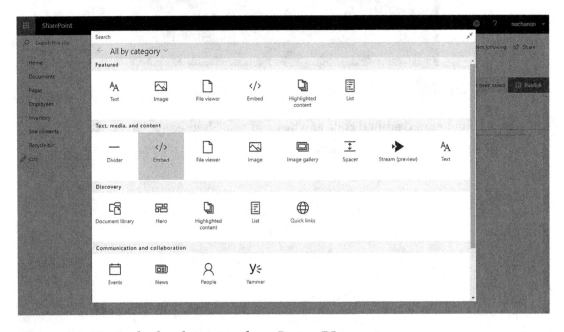

Embed code

Link you can send in email

https://app.powerbi.com/view?r=eyJrljoiOGNjYjUxMDYtZjI2Yi00Yzg5LTk0N2MtNz

Html you can paste into your blog or website

<iframe width="800" height="600" src="https://app.powerbi.com/view?r=eyJrljoi

Size   800 x 600 px   ▼

Close

Figure 16-18. *Embed code for a published Power BI report*

3. Open a **SharePoint Online** site. Add the **Embed** web part
    (Figure 16-19).

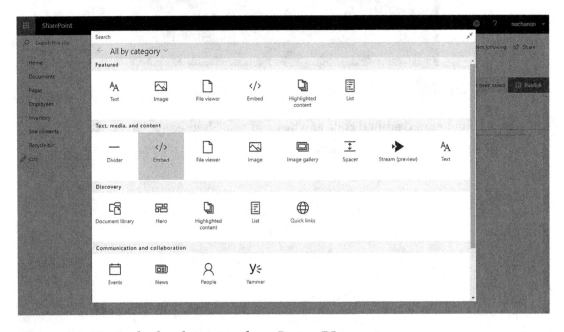

Figure 16-19. *Embed web part to show Power BI report*

4. Copy the embed code to the web part property (Figure 16-20).

Figure 16-20. *Power BI embed code*

5. You can also use the **Power BI** web part under the **Business and intelligence** category to show the Power BI report by specifying the published report URL (Figure 16-21).

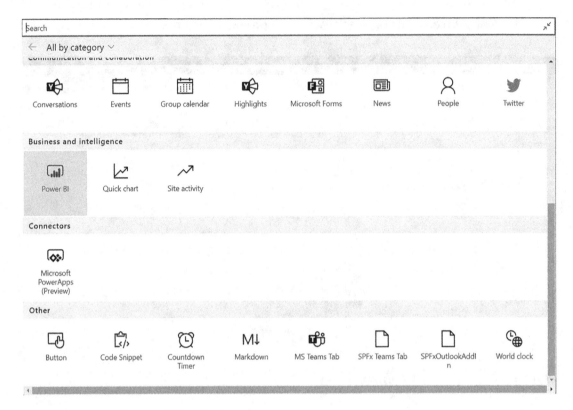

Figure 16-21. *Power BI embed code*

The on-premises (SharePoint Server 2019) data now can be seen in the cloud (SharePoint Online site).

Scheduling a Refresh of Datasets

You should define the schedule for refreshing the datasets from SharePoint Server 2019 to get the latest data from the data source. Follow these steps to schedule a refresh of datasets:

1. Under **My workspace**, click **Data sets**.

2. Select the dataset (e.g. Inventory).

3. Under **Scheduled refresh**, define the refresh schedule (Figure 16-22).

Figure 16-22. *Scheduled refresh of datasets*

Conclusion

The Power BI reporting cloud feature is available in SharePoint Server 2019. An on-premises data gateway helps to connect to on-premises data sources. The Embed and Power BI web parts in SharePoint Online help to display the published Power BI reports, getting the data from on-premises datasets using the on-premises data gateway. Schedule periodic refreshes of datasets to get updated data from the datasets.

In the next chapter, you will explore how to integrate Power Apps with SharePoint Server 2019 on-premises using the gateway.

CHAPTER 17

Power Apps Integration with SharePoint Server 2019

SharePoint Server 2019 offers various new features. Power Apps integration is one of the features that bring the cloud experience on-premises. Power Apps help users design custom apps for business needs by connecting to various sources or data platforms. In this chapter, you will explore how to integrate Power Apps with SharePoint Server 2019 on-premises using a data gateway.

Power Apps Overview

Power Apps helps users build custom apps without writing any code. Power Apps have a responsive design and work well in browsers and on mobile devices. There are two types of Power Apps:

1. **Canvas apps:** They provide the flexibility to arrange the user experience and interface the way you want to configure it. You can start creating a canvas app from a blank canvas, data, sample, or common data service source.

2. **Model-driven apps:** They can be created from the Power Apps site. They help to rapidly develop forms, business rules, and process flows by using a common data service.

© Nanddeep Sadanand Nachan and Smita Sadanand Nachan 2020
N. S. Nachan and S. S. Nachan, *Understanding Hybrid Environments in SharePoint 2019*,
https://doi.org/10.1007/978-1-4842-6050-0_17

Note   In SharePoint Server 2019, it is possible to use Power Apps in a hybrid environment. First, you must set up a data gateway. Follow the instructions from Chapter 15 to install and configure a data gateway.

Building a Power Apps Canvas App

Follow these steps to build a Power Apps canvas app:

1. Sign into **Power Apps** (https://web.powerapps.com).

2. On the Home screen, under **Start from data**, click **SharePoint**. (Figure 17-1).

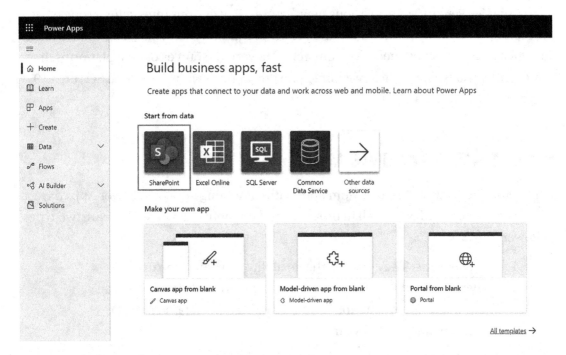

Figure 17-1. *Starting from SharePoint data*

3. Under **Connections**, click **New connection** (Figure 17-2).

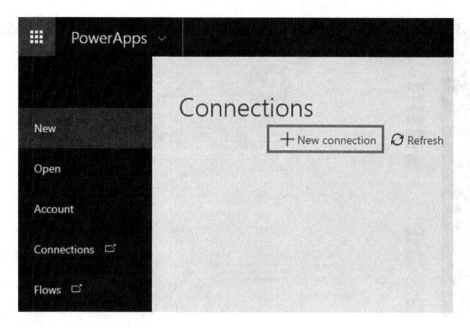

Figure 17-2. *New connection*

4. From the available list of connections, select **SharePoint**.

5. Select **Connect using on-premises data gateway**.

6. Select the **Authentication** type as **Windows**.

7. Specify the username and password to get connected to your SharePoint Server 2019 on-premises farm.

8. Select the gateway to use from the list.

9. Click **Create** (Figure 17-3).

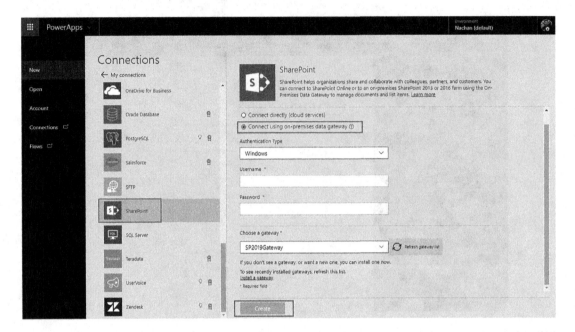

Figure 17-3. *Creating a new SharePoint connection*

10. Specify the SharePoint site URL to connect to.

11. Click **Go** (Figure 17-4).

Figure 17-4. *Connecting to the SharePoint site*

12. Select the list to connect to or enter a custom list name to create it.
     For this demonstration, select the preexisting **Employees** list.

13. Click **Connect** (Figure 17-5).

Figure 17-5. *Choosing a SharePoint list*

14. The app is ready to configure. BrowseScreen1 will help to configure the All items view. DetailScreen1 will help to configure the View item screen. EditScreen1 will help to configure the Edit item screen (Figure 17-6).

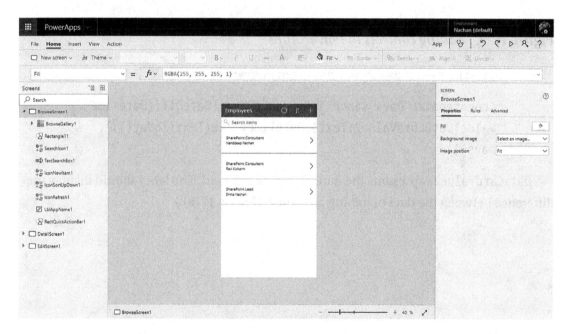

Figure 17-6. *Configuring screens*

15. Open **DetailScreen1** to modify it.

16. Click **Insert ➤ Text ➤ Label** (Figure 17-7).

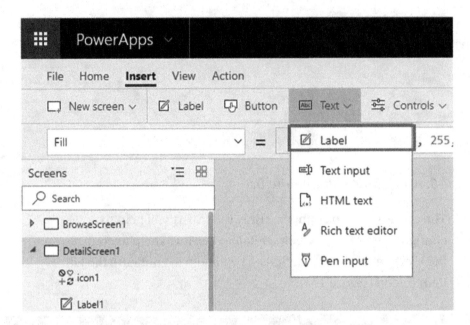

Figure 17-7. *Adding controls to Power Apps*

17. Type in the text as formula as shown below:

```
Concatenate("Days since joined: ", Text(DateDiff(DateTime
Value(DataCardValue2.Text),DateTimeValue(Text(Today())),
Days)))
```

DataCardValue2 represents the date of joining the field. The label should display the difference between the date of joining and today (Figure 17-8).

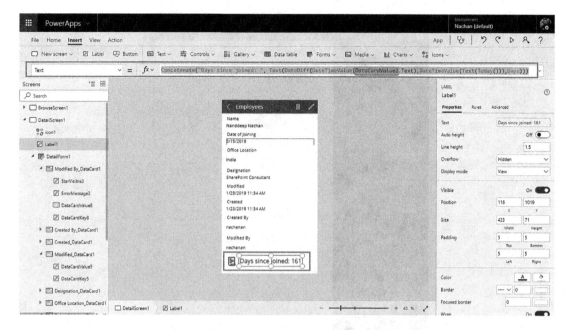

Figure 17-8. *Configuring controls for Power Apps*

Publishing the Power Apps App

Follow these steps to publish the app built with Power Apps:

1. Click **File ➤ Save ➤ The Cloud**.

2. Click **Save** (Figure 17-9).

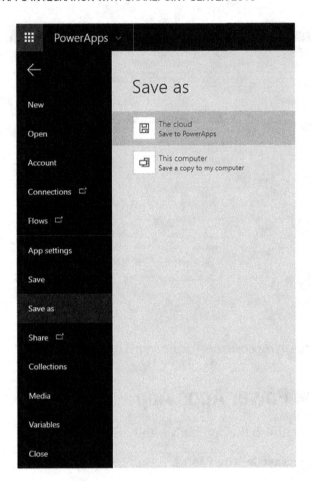

Figure 17-9. *Publishing the Power Apps app*

3.   Click **Share this app** (Figure 17-10).

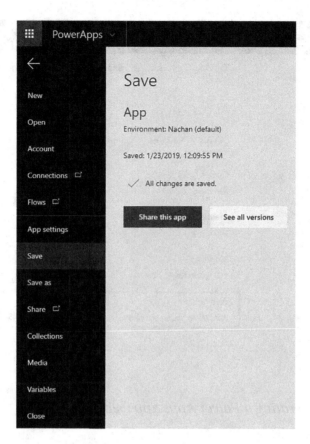

Figure 17-10. *Sharing the Power Apps app*

    4.   The app can be accessed from a web link URL (Figure 17-11).

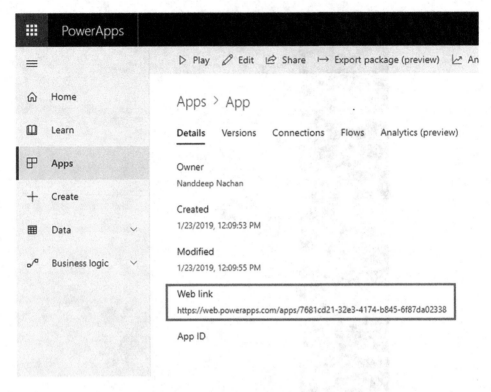

Figure 17-11. *Generating a Power Apps app web link*

Showcasing the Power Apps App in SharePoint Online

Follow these steps to display your custom business app in SharePoint Online:

1. Open the **SharePoint Online** site.

2. Edit the page and add the **Microsoft Power Apps (Preview)** web part under the **Connectors** category (Figure 17-12).

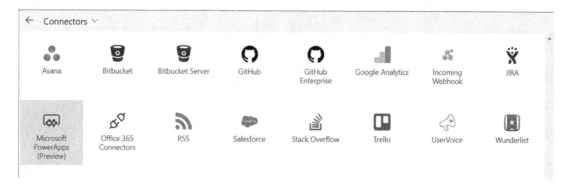

Figure 17-12. *Power Apps web part in SharePoint Online*

3. Edit the web part and add an app web link or ID to the web part property (Figure 17-13).

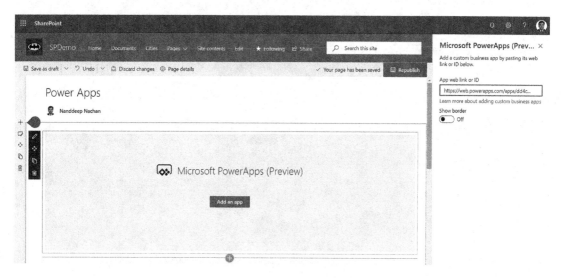

Figure 17-13. *Specifying an app web link or ID to the web part property*

Conclusion

The Power Apps feature brings the cloud experience to SharePoint Server 2019 on-premises. You can set up a data gateway for creating canvas apps. Power Apps offer a responsive design and work well in browsers and on mobile devices. SharePoint Online provides the Microsoft Power Apps (Preview) web part to render the Power Apps apps in a browser.

In the next chapter, you will explore how to integrate Power Automate with SharePoint Server 2019 on-premises using a gateway.

CHAPTER 18

Power Automate Integration with SharePoint Server 2019

Power Automate integration is one of the cloud features that made it on-premises with SharePoint Server 2019. Microsoft Flow helped to automate tasks by connecting to various systems; Power Automate offers the flexibility to go beyond creating traditional SharePoint-centric workflows by connecting to various services. Power Automate widens the opportunities for SharePoint users to automate their processes. In this chapter, you will explore how to integrate Power Automate with SharePoint Server 2019 on-premises using a data gateway.

Note   In SharePoint Server 2019, it is possible to use Power Automate in a hybrid environment. First, you must set up a data gateway. Follow the instructions from Chapter 15 to install and configure the data gateway.

Power Automate Overview

Power Automate (once called MS Flow) is Microsoft's cloud-based workflow tool. It helps to automate tasks by connecting to various sources across Microsoft 365 and beyond. It automates any repetitive, time consuming, or approval-based tasks. It comes with ready-to-use templates and recommendations.

© Nanddeep Sadanand Nachan and Smita Sadanand Nachan 2020
N. S. Nachan and S. S. Nachan, *Understanding Hybrid Environments in SharePoint 2019,*
https://doi.org/10.1007/978-1-4842-6050-0_18

There are three types of Power Automate flows:

- **Automated flow:** Gets activated when a preselected event occurs (e.g. a file is uploaded).

- **Scheduled flow:** Occurs at a specified time (e.g. a notification on a daily basis).

- **Button flow:** Triggered by the press of a button.

Configuring a Power Automate Connection

Power Automate helps to automate tasks with connected sources. SharePoint is one of them.

Follow these steps to configure a Power Automate connection to SharePoint:

1. Sign into **Power Automate** (`https://flow.microsoft.com`).

2. On the Home screen, click the **Gear icon** and select **Connections** (Figure 18-1).

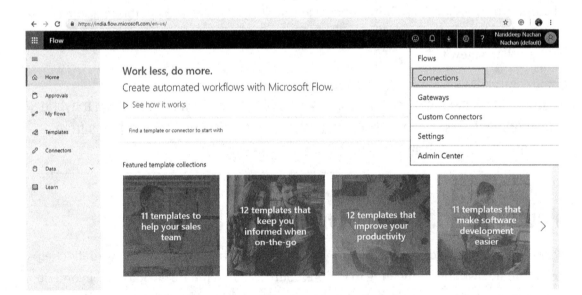

Figure 18-1. *Browsing Power Automate connections*

3. The page displays the earlier setup connections. Click **New connection** (Figure 18-2).

Figure 18-2. *Creating a new Power Automate connection*

4. Select **SharePoint** from the connections list.

5. Select **Connect using on-premises data gateway**.

6. Select **Windows Authentication**. Provide a username and password to connect to the SharePoint Server 2019 farm.

7. Choose the installed gateway.

8. Click **Create** (Figure 18-3).

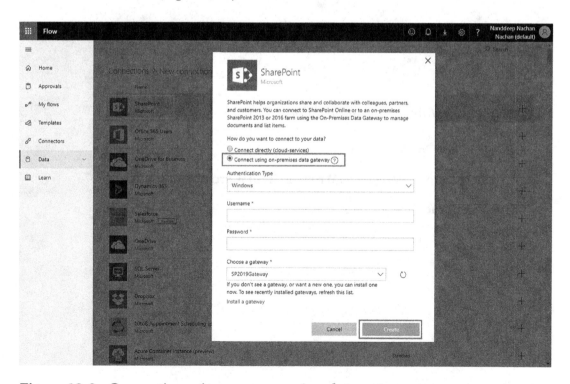

Figure 18-3. *Connecting using an on-premises data gateway*

217

Creating Microsoft Flow

As an example, you will take a simple scenario of an email being triggered to Office 365 Outlook when an item is added or updated in the SharePoint 2019 on-premises environment. Once the connection is ready, follow these steps to create Power Automate:

1. Click **Create** from the left menu.

2. Select **Automated flow** (Figure 18-4).

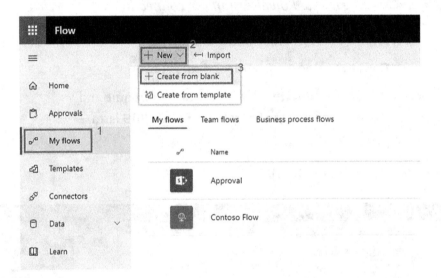

Figure 18-4. *Creating an automated flow*

3. Name the flow.

4. Choose the flow trigger as **When an item is created or modified**.

5. Click **Create** (Figure 18-5).

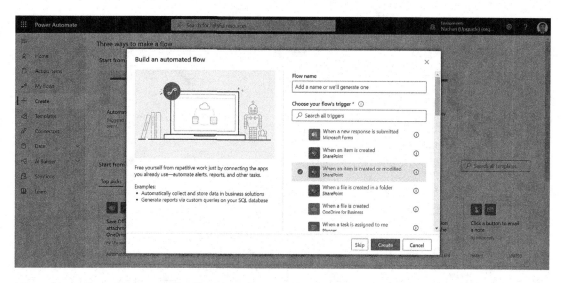

Figure 18-5. *Choosing the flow's trigger*

6. Click the menu and select **SharePoint Server 2019 connection**
   out of all available connections (Figure 18-6).

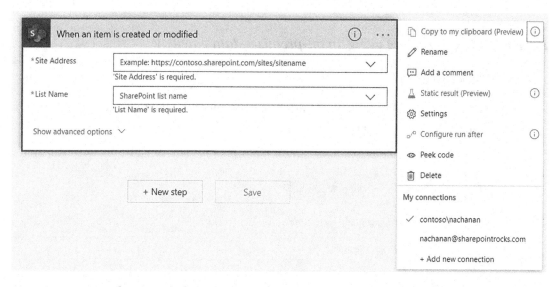

Figure 18-6. *Selecting a SharePoint Server 2019 on-premises connection*

7. For first-time use, create a connection by clicking **+ Add new
   connection**.

8. Select the on-premises gateway option. Provide the Windows
   authentication credentials (Figure 18-7).

219

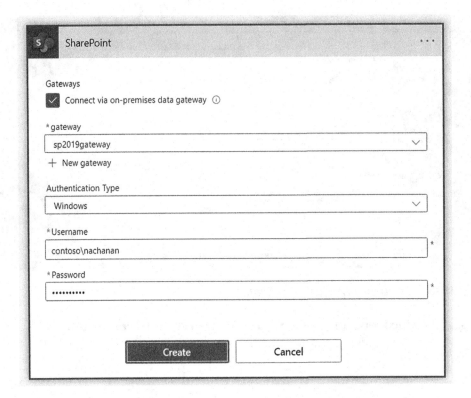

Figure 18-7. *Connecting using an on-premises data gateway*

9.   Click **Create**.

10.   Enter the SharePoint 2019 site address and select the list to run the
      Power Automate on (Figure 18-8).

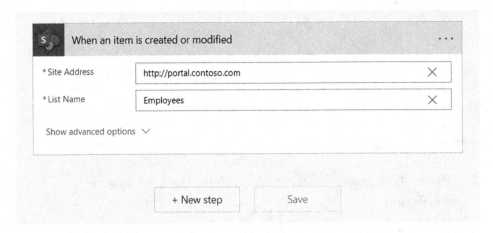

Figure 18-8. *Connecting to a SharePoint Server 2019 site and list*

11.   Click **New step**.

12.   Select **Mail**.

13.   Under **actions**, select **Send an email notification (V3)** (Figure 18-9).

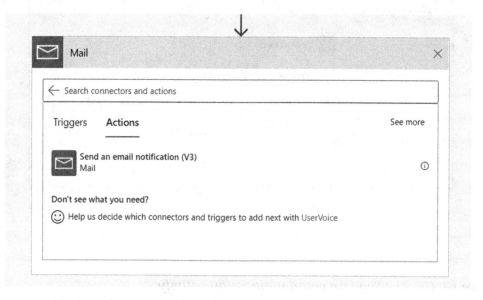

Figure 18-9. *Sending an email notification*

14.   Compose the email to, subject, and body.

15.   Click **Save** (Figure 18-10).

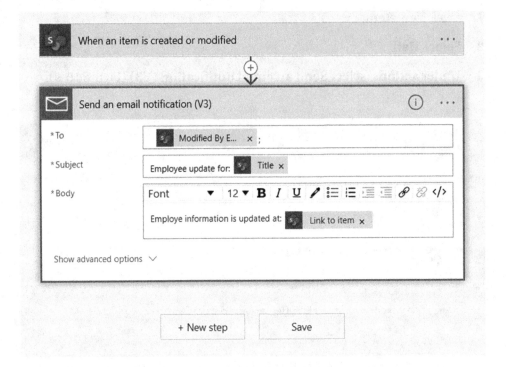

Figure 18-10. *The Send an email notification activity*

Testing the Power Automate

Follow these steps to test the created Power Automate:

1. Click **Test**.

2. Select **I'll perform the trigger action** (Figure 18-11).

Figure 18-11. *Testing the flow*

3. Click **Save and test**.

4. Open the SharePoint list and add a new item.

5. Wait until the flow finishes (Figure 18-12).

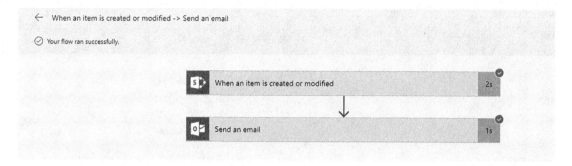

Figure 18-12. *Flow run progress*

6. Check Office 365 Outlook for an email generated from Power Automate (Figure 18-13).

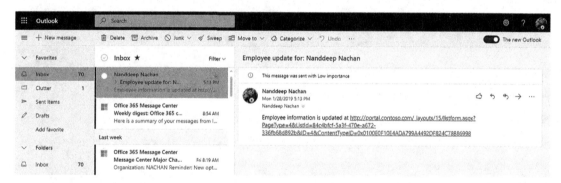

Figure 18-13. *Validating the flow*

Conclusion

Power Automate helps to automate business processes. This chapter demonstrated the simple scenario of communicating with SharePoint Server 2019 on-premises from the cloud using an on-premises data gateway. In a similar way, complex business processes can be automated using Power Automate.

In the next chapter, you will explore Office Online Server for SharePoint Server 2019, which allows users to read and edit the Microsoft Office documents in a browser.

CHAPTER 19

Office Online Server for SharePoint Server 2019

SharePoint is mostly known for document collaboration. End users manage documents in SharePoint. Viewing and editing the documents in a browser experience is a more preferred option rather than downloading a copy of the document and working on it.

SharePoint Online offers inline editing functionality out of the box. However, when it comes to the SharePoint on-premises environment, in the past (SharePoint 2013 days) we had to install Office Web Apps for this purpose. Later, in SharePoint 2016, Office Online Server (OOS) was introduced. OOS is the successor to Office Web Apps Server 2013. SharePoint 2019 continues to use OOS.

Introduction to Office Online Server

Office Online Server is the next version/successor of Office Web Apps. It allows users to read and edit Microsoft Office documents in the browser. SharePoint Server 2016 and 2019's Durable Links feature requires OOS as a prerequisite.

OOS needs to be installed on a separate server. It cannot be installed on the same server where SharePoint Server 2019 is installed.

Downloading and Installing Office Online Server

Microsoft has made Office Online Server available to MSDN subscribers. Earlier it was only available to volume licensing customers.

© Nanddeep Sadanand Nachan and Smita Sadanand Nachan 2020
N. S. Nachan and S. S. Nachan, *Understanding Hybrid Environments in SharePoint 2019*,
https://doi.org/10.1007/978-1-4842-6050-0_19

Note   As of today, OOS is available for subscriptions including Visual Studio Enterprise Volume Licensing, Visual Studio Enterprise with GitHub Enterprise, and Visual Studio Enterprise Annual.

As mentioned, you must set up a separate server for installing OOS. It could be a Windows Server 2012 R2. Download the **Office Online Server** binaries to the server from your Visual Studio subscription.

If you double-click to install it, you may get the error message shown in Figure 19-1.

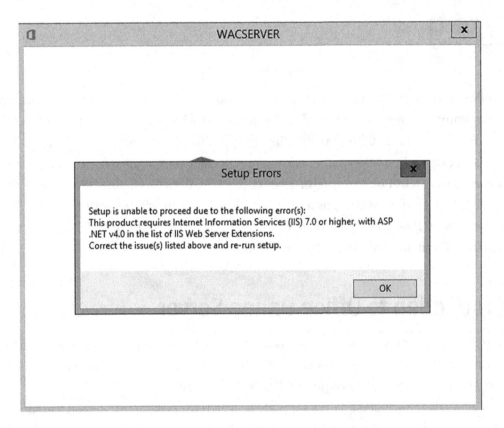

Figure 19-1. *Office Online Server setup error*

As per the error message, you must enable the Web-Server role on the server to install OOS.

Option 1: Graphical Interface: You may use a graphical interface to install this feature. Follow these instructions to install OOS using the GUI feature:

1. Launch **Server Manager.**

2. Click **Manage ➤ Add Roles and Features** (Figure 19-2).

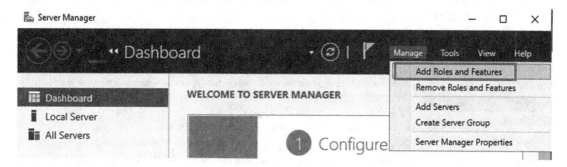

Figure 19-2. *Adding roles and features*

3. Click **Next** to continue (Figure 19-3).

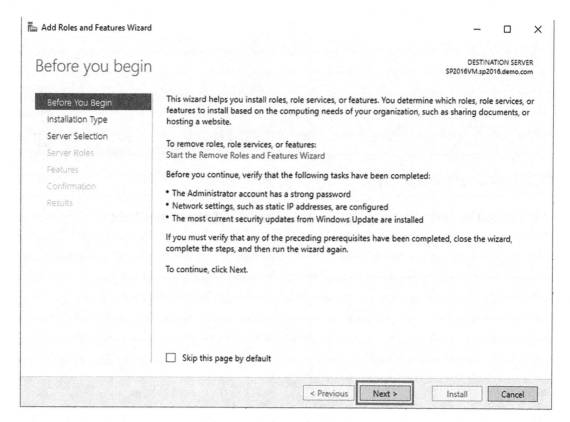

Figure 19-3. *The Add Roles and Features Wizard*

4. In the installation type, select **Role-based or feature-based installation**. Click **Next** (Figure 19-4).

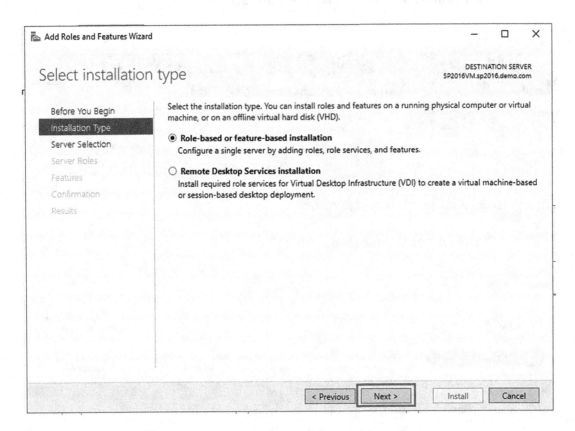

Figure 19-4. *Installation type*

5. Select the local server where you want to install OOS. Click **Next** (Figure 19-5).

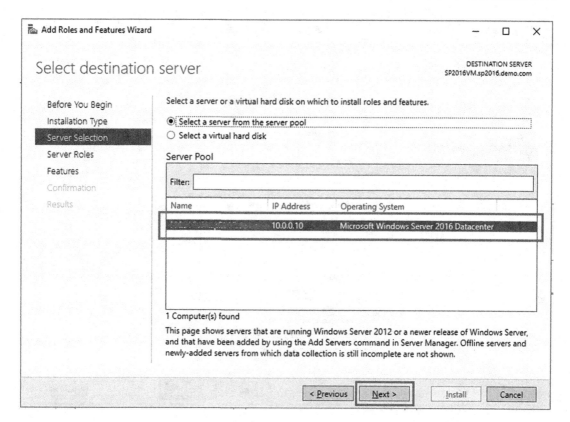

Figure 19-5. *Server selection*

6. In the **Server Roles,** select **Web Server (IIS).** Click **Next** (Figure 19-6).

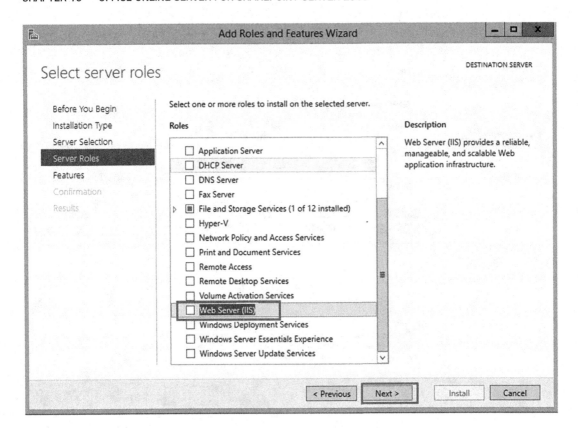

Figure 19-6. *Web Server (IIS) role*

7. Review and click **Add Features** to proceed (Figure 19-7).

Figure 19-7. *Adding the Web Server (IIS) role*

8. In the **Features** section, select **Ink and Handwriting Services.**
    Click **Next** (Figure 19-8).

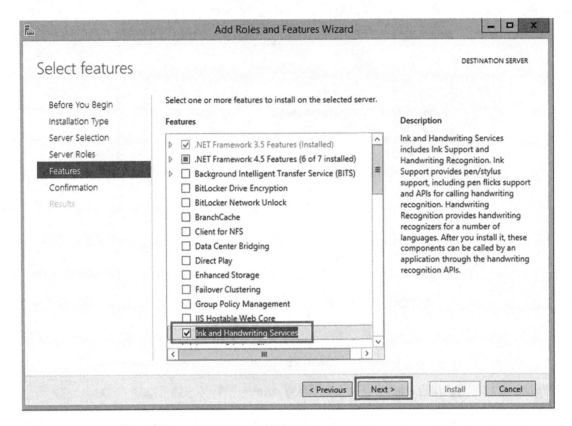

Figure 19-8. *Ink and handwriting services*

9. In the **Web Server Role (IIS)** screen, click **Next.**

10. In the **Select role services** screen, keep the default options selected and click **Next.**

11. In the **Confirm installation selections** screen, click **Install.**

12. Once the installation finishes, close the window.

Option 2: PowerShell Cmdlet

1. Open **Windows PowerShell** with administrative privileges.

2. Run **the following** command:

```
Install-WindowsFeature -Name Web-Server,
InkAndHandWritingServices -IncludeAllSubFeature
```

Installing Office Online Server

Once the required Windows feature is installed, try installing the Office Online Server again by double-clicking the binaries downloaded from MSDN.

Follow these steps to install the Office Online Server:

1.   Click **I accept the terms of this agreement** and click **Continue** (Figure 19-9).

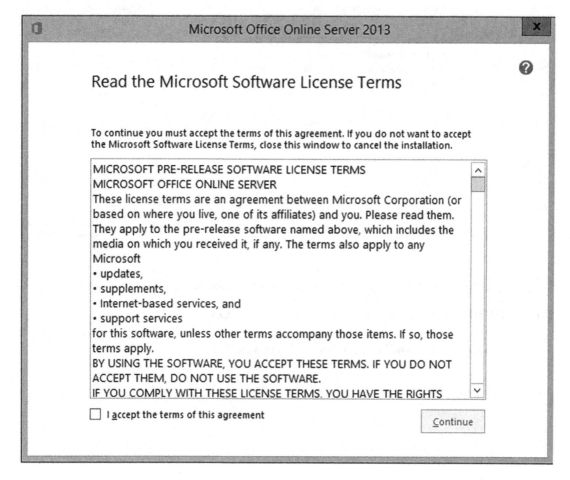

Figure 19-9. *Microsoft Office Online Server installation*

2.   Go ahead with the default installation path, unless you desire to change it.

3.   Click **Install Now** (Figure 19-10).

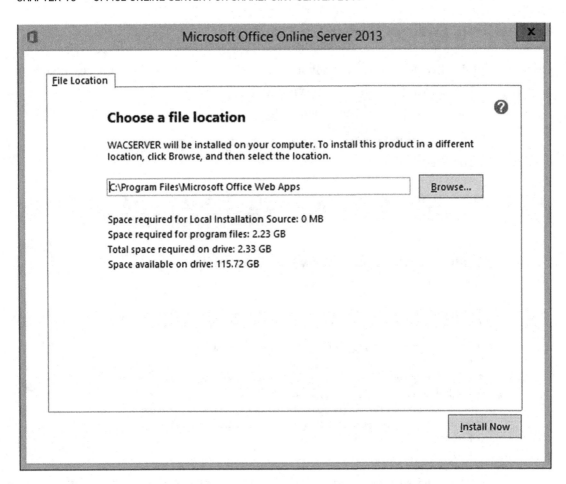

Figure 19-10. *Choosing a file location to install OOS*

4.   Wait for the installation to finish (Figure 19-11).

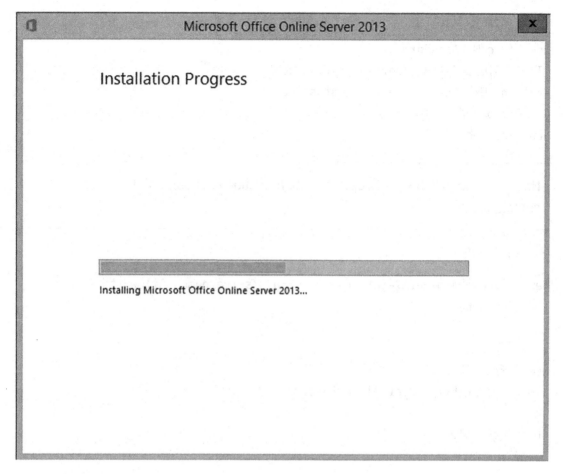

Figure 19-11. *Microsoft Office Online Server installation*

5. Once finished installing, click **Close.**

Setting Up an Office Online Farm

Use the following PowerShell to install the module needed to set up the Office Online farm:

```
Import-Module OfficeWebApp
```

For HTTPS:

```
New-OfficeWebAppsFarm -InternalUrl "HTTPS Url" -ExternalUrl "HTTPS Url"
-SSLOffloaded -EditingEnabled
```

Example:

```
New-OfficeWebAppsFarm
-InternalUrl "http://portal.contoso.com"
-ExternalUrl "http://portal.contoso.com"
-SSLOffloaded
-EditingEnabled
```

Note   Do not use SSLOffloaded in a production environment if you prefer SSL communication.

For HTTP:

```
New-OfficeWebAppsFarm -InternalURL http://servername -AllowHttp
-EditingEnabled
```

Example:

```
New-OfficeWebAppsFarm
-InternalURL http://portal.contoso.com
-AllowHttp
-EditingEnabled
```

Verifying If the Office Online Server Is Working

To test the setup, try accessing the following URL from any browser:

```
http://<server name>/hosting/discovery
```

If everything is ok, the browser will display XML like in Figure 19-12.

```
<?xml version="1.0" encoding="UTF-8"?>
- <wopi-discovery>
  - <net-zone name="internal-https">
    - <app name="Excel" checkLicense="true"
      favIconUrl="https://oos.contoso.com/x/_layouts/images/FavIcon_Excel.ico">
        <action name="view" urlsrc="https://oos.contoso.com/x/_layouts/xlviewerinternal.aspx?
          <ui=UI_LLCC&><rs=DC_LLCC&>" default="true" ext="ods"/>
        <action name="view" urlsrc="https://oos.contoso.com/x/_layouts/xlviewerinternal.aspx?
          <ui=UI_LLCC&><rs=DC_LLCC&>" default="true" ext="xls"/>
        <action name="view" urlsrc="https://oos.contoso.com/x/_layouts/xlviewerinternal.aspx?
          <ui=UI_LLCC&><rs=DC_LLCC&>" default="true" ext="xlsb"/>
        <action name="view" urlsrc="https://oos.contoso.com/x/_layouts/xlviewerinternal.aspx?
          <ui=UI_LLCC&><rs=DC_LLCC&>" default="true" ext="xlsm"/>
        <action name="view" urlsrc="https://oos.contoso.com/x/_layouts/xlviewerinternal.aspx?
          <ui=UI_LLCC&><rs=DC_LLCC&>" default="true" ext="xlsx"/>
        <action name="edit" urlsrc="https://oos.contoso.com/x/_layouts/xlviewerinternal.aspx?
          edit=1&<ui=UI_LLCC&><rs=DC_LLCC&>" ext="ods" requires="update"/>
        <action name="edit" urlsrc="https://oos.contoso.com/x/_layouts/xlviewerinternal.aspx?
          edit=1&<ui=UI_LLCC&><rs=DC_LLCC&>" ext="xlsb" requires="update"/>
        <action name="edit" urlsrc="https://oos.contoso.com/x/_layouts/xlviewerinternal.aspx?
          edit=1&<ui=UI_LLCC&><rs=DC_LLCC&>" ext="xlsm" requires="update"/>
        <action name="edit" urlsrc="https://oos.contoso.com/x/_layouts/xlviewerinternal.aspx?
          edit=1&<ui=UI_LLCC&><rs=DC_LLCC&>" ext="xlsx" requires="update"/>
        <action name="editnew" urlsrc="https://oos.contoso.com/x/_layouts/xlviewerinternal.aspx?
          edit=1&new=1&<ui=UI_LLCC&><rs=DC_LLCC&>" ext="xlsx" requires="update"/>
        <action name="interactivepreview" urlsrc="https://oos.contoso.com/x/_layouts/xlpreview.aspx?
          <ui=UI_LLCC&><rs=DC_LLCC&>" ext="xlsb"/>
        <action name="interactivepreview" urlsrc="https://oos.contoso.com/x/_layouts/xlpreview.aspx?
          <ui=UI_LLCC&><rs=DC_LLCC&>" ext="xlsm"/>
```

Figure 19-12. *WOPI discovery XML*

Connecting to a SharePoint Server 2019 Farm

You must now link the Office Online Server to the SharePoint Server 2019 farm by using the following PowerShell command:

```
New-SPWOPIBinding -ServerName <servername> -AllowHTTP
```

Example:

```
New-SPWOPIBinding
-ServerName "SP2019"
-AllowHTTP
```

You are now all set to experience the browser experience for Office documents.

Conclusion

Office Online Server enables the inline viewing and editing experience for SharePoint on-premises users. OOS is the successor to Office Web Apps Server 2013. It needs to be installed on a separate server.

In the next chapter, you will explore high-level scenarios of upgrading to SharePoint Server 2019 from prior SharePoint on-premises versions.

CHAPTER 20

SharePoint Server 2019 Upgrade Scenarios

As a SharePoint administrator and developer, you support customer portals on various on-premises versions of SharePoint, such as SharePoint 2010, 2013, or 2016. (Microsoft Office SharePoint Server 2007 (a.k.a. MOSS) reached the end of support in October 2017.) You always strive to build future-proof SharePoint solutions that will support upcoming versions of SharePoint but every new release of SharePoint prompts you to upgrade to it.

In this chapter, you will explore high-level scenarios of upgrading to SharePoint Server 2019 from prior SharePoint on-premises versions.

Upgrade Scenarios

Upgrading from SharePoint Server 2016: The upgrade scenario from SharePoint Server 2016 has not changed. Like previous version upgrades, SharePoint Server 2019 supports a direct upgrade from its immediate predecessor (SharePoint Server 2016). The database should be a SharePoint 2016 RTM or higher version to upgrade to SharePoint Server 2019.

Upgrading from SharePoint 2013: There is no direct upgrade path from SharePoint 2013 to 2019. You must first upgrade to SharePoint Server 2016 and then upgrade to SharePoint Server 2019 (Figure 20-1).

© Nanddeep Sadanand Nachan and Smita Sadanand Nachan 2020
N. S. Nachan and S. S. Nachan, *Understanding Hybrid Environments in SharePoint 2019*,
https://doi.org/10.1007/978-1-4842-6050-0_20

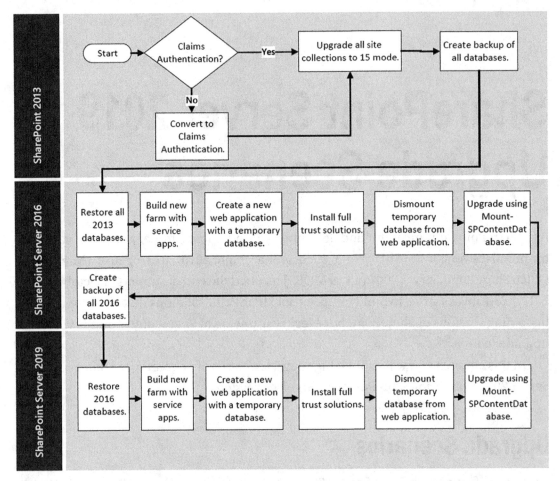

Figure 20-1. *SharePoint upgrade scenarios Image source: docs.microsoft.com*

The following service applications have databases that can be upgraded:

- User Profile Service application

- Search Service application

- The Managed Metadata Service application

- The Secure Store Service application

- Business Data Connectivity Service application

- PerformancePoint Services Service application

High-Level Upgrade Scenarios

Upgrading from SharePoint 2013 to SharePoint 2016: Upgrading from SharePoint 2013 to SharePoint Server 2019 requires an upgrade to SharePoint Server 2016 first. SharePoint Server 2016 cannot be skipped in a migration path. These points need to be considered/carried out on SharePoint 2013:

- SharePoint Server 2016 and 2019 by default support claims authentication. However, SharePoint 2013 supported Windows authentication as the default mode. Therefore, the web applications in Windows authentication should be first converted to claims authentication.

- All site collections should be upgraded from 14 mode to 15 mode by using the **Upgrade-SPSite** cmdlet.

- Back up all content and service application databases from SharePoint 2013 (SQL Server) and restore to SharePoint Server 2016 (SQL Server).

The following points need to be considered/carried out on SharePoint Server 2016:

- Set up a SharePoint Server 2016 farm. For setting up a service application database, use the one restored from SharePoint 2013.

- Create new web applications with the temporary database.

- Install full trust solutions, if any.

- Dismount temporary databases from web applications. Upgrade restored content databases by running the **Mount-SPContentDatabase** cmdlet.

- Perform additional configuration changes that are not part of service applications and content databases (e.g. incoming/outgoing email settings, etc.).

Upgrading from SharePoint Server 2016 to SharePoint Server 2019: Upgrading from SharePoint Server 2016 to SharePoint Server 2019 is relatively simpler and straightforward as compared to upgrading from SharePoint 2013 to SharePoint Server 2016 due to the following reasons:

241

- Claims authentication is the default mode in both SharePoint Server 2016 and 2019. This reduces the burden of converting the authentication mode.

- Upgrading databases mode to level 15 is not needed.

The following points need to be considered/carried out on SharePoint 2016:

- Back up all content and service application databases from SharePoint Server 2016 (SQL Server).

- Restore these databases to SharePoint Server 2019 (SQL Server).

The following points need to be considered/carried out on SharePoint 2019:

- Set up a SharePoint Server 2019 farm. For setting up a service application database, use the one restored from SharePoint Server 2016.

- Create new web applications with the temporary database.

- Install full trust solutions, if any.

- Dismount temporary databases from web applications. Upgrade restored content databases by running the **Mount-SPContentDatabase** cmdlet.

- Perform additional configuration changes that are not part of service applications and content databases (e.g. incoming/outgoing email settings, etc.)

References

Here are some reference links that will help your journey to upgrade from previous versions of SharePoint to SharePoint Serer 2019:

- Upgrade to SharePoint Server 2019 (https://docs.microsoft.com/en-us/sharepoint/upgrade-and-update/upgrade-to-sharepoint-server-2019)

- Overview of the upgrade process to SharePoint Server 2019 (`https://docs.microsoft.com/en-us/sharepoint/upgrade-and-update/overview-of-the-upgrade-process-2019`)

- High-level overview to upgrade from SharePoint 2013 to SharePoint Server 2019 (`https://docs.microsoft.com/en-us/sharepoint/upgrade-and-update/upgrade-from-sharepoint2013-to-sharepointserver-2019`)

Conclusion

Scenarios for an upgrade to SharePoint Server 2019 have not changed. SharePoint Server 2019 supports a direct upgrade from its immediate predecessor, SharePoint Server 2016. Upgrading from SharePoint Server 2016 to 2019 is straightforward, considering both use claims authentication and the default mode of 15.

Index

A, B

C, D, E

© Nanddeep Sadanand Nachan and Smita Sadanand Nachan 2020
N. S. Nachan and S. S. Nachan, *Understanding Hybrid Environments in SharePoint 2019*,
https://doi.org/10.1007/978-1-4842-6050-0

P, Q

*vs.*SharePoint Server 2016, 48

software requirements, 8, 9

Trial VM (*see* Trial VM, MS Azure)

VM setup options

    data server, 9

    plain vanilla installation, 9

    Trial VM, 10

sp_PortalAppPool, 27

T

Trial VM, MS Azure

    configuration, 15, 16

    connection, 19

    creation information, 12, 17, 18

    deployment completion, 18, 19

    disk type, 13

    informations, 11

    locating, 10, 11

management options, 14, 15

network configurations, 13, 14

resources, 16, 17

U, V, W, X, Y, Z

UPN suffix

    Office 365, 84, 85

    single user, 85, 86

User experience

    Communication sites, 34, 35

    lists/libraries experienece, 32, 33

    pages/web parts, 36

    search experience, 37, 38

    site collection creation, 31, 32

    site contents, 38

    site usage, 39

    team sites, 33